D1050458

Shattered Soul?

Five Pathways to Healing the Spirit after Abuse and Trauma

*Blessings, Jamie!
And all the best to you
in your work and
ministry.*

Vicki Schmidt

WordStream
Publishing

Copyright ©2011
WordStream Publishing, LLC Nashville, Tennessee
www.WordStreamPublishing.com

First paperback edition: September 2011

Trade Edition paperback ISBN 9781935758082/ ebook 9781935758099

All rights reserved. No part of this publication may be reproduced, stored in a retrieval
system, or transmitted, in any form or by any means, electronic, mechanical, photocopying,
recoding, or otherwise, without the prior written permission of WordStream Publishing, LLC.

Unless otherwise indicated, all Scripture texts in this work are taken from the New
American Bible with Revised New Testament and Revised Psalms ©1991, 1986, 1970
Confraternity of Christian Doctrine, Washington, D.C., and are used by permission of
the copyright owner. All Rights Reserved. No part of the New American Bible may be
reproduced in any form without permission in writing from the copyright owner.

Interior Design: Rob Williams
Editor: April Benson

1 2 3 4 5 6 7 8 9 10

Printed in the United States of America

We dedicate this book to everyone who is caught in the cycle of abuse. May the cycle be broken with healing for all.

With the drawing of this Love and the voice of this Calling
We shall not cease from exploration
And the end of all our exploring
Will be to arrive where we started
And know the place for the first time.
—from T. S. Eliot's *Four Quartets*

Table of Contents

Acknowledgements

Thank You, God, for this opportunity to journey so intimately with my best friend, co-author, challenger, adventurer, spiritual mentor and husband, Patrick. He is truly open to your Spirit and to allowing the "writer" to be heard! For this I am grateful.

And where would I be without my children, Joe, Mary, Gerry, Cindy and Louise, and their amazing spouses, Ken, Angie, Arnie, and Jack? From the time they were little I have learned from my children, laughed and cried with them, and I continue to be humbled by their unconditional love for me. Thank you! Jason, Molly, Christopher, John, Sammi, Michelle, Nicole, Kevin, Maggie, Erin and Kate, you are the best grandchildren, and the icing on the cake is my two great grandchildren, Emery and Belle. All of you bring smiles, joy, wonderment, new perspectives, challenge, excitement, awe, hugs, and lots of love. Each one of you is a sacred blessing and creates life and joy in me. As a woman of strength and courage, I thank my family, my dear friends, and all those who have gone before me for the model you have provided in responding to the challenge called life. All of these relationships and inspirations, and everything that I have learned from my clients, especially my fellow survivors, have brought me to this sacred place of being me—for today.

Vicki, I am very grateful that you joined us in the healing work of this book. Thank you for having the courage to share your sacred story of triumph over abuse. Thank you, Marti Williams, our publisher. You are truly a breathe of fresh air! You have been inspirational, visionary, creative, and fun all through the process of birthing this book. It has been a great learning experience to journey with you as we choose to trust you with our sacred treasure, Shattered Soul? Thanks for partnering with us.

Life is great—change is constant—and love flows from heart to heart.
—Sue Lauber-Fleming

In this twenty-year journey of healing, I give grateful thanks to Sue Lauber-Fleming for seeing something in me that I could not see. Sue saw that bright light in me and patiently led me to see it too. She is a gifted woman, a teacher of hard-won wisdom, a lover of life. Sue, I count you among my most precious friends. Thanks also to Patrick Fleming for his dear friendship and encouragement to be a part of this book. It is such a privilege to write with you and Sue. From the early days of my healing process, I thank Paul and Judy Kren, Mary Beth Bux, O.S.F., Barbara Erdman, and my dear family. Their love and support was mammoth, and buoyed me when I was sinking and did not think that I could move onward. Today, I am very grateful to Barbara Fuhrwerk for her friendship and her coaching about my writing, and to Barbara Blesse, O.P., for her friendship and assistance in editing my contribution to Shattered Soul?

—Vicki Schmidt

Words cannot express the gratefulness that I feel to Sue, my best friend, wife, my anam-cara, partner, co-therapist, and once again co-author. Thank you, Sue, for the many years of fun, adventure, spiritual journeying, support, challenge, work, and love that we have shared. I am grateful too, for your patience and willingness to be an "author's widow" during several periods of the past two years. Soul-felt thanks to Vicki Schmidt for her willingness to share her journey of courage, healing, and great soul with us in life and in this book. I am very grateful to the five anonymous contributors to Shattered Soul? whose writings and reflections about their pilgrimage of spiritual healing also helped to bring the ideas of this book to life in a very personal way.

I want to thank our former editor, Roy M. Carlisle, for his early support and encouragement for this book. Thanks as well to Paula D'Arcy for her instrumental belief in our work and writing, and for capturing so well the spirit of the book in her foreword. I feel great appreciation for our present publisher, Marti Williams of WordStream Publishing, for her boundless enthusiasm and creativity in helping to bring the book to life. Thanks to our editor, April Benson, and the rest of the WordStream team, whose insights and contributions added much to the final product. I also want to express my gratefulness to the monks of Nada Hermitage in Crestone, Colorado and to the Companions in Infinite Love at Windridge Solitude in Lonedell, Missouri for your prayers and support, and for providing such wonderfully peaceful and contemplative environments in which to pray and write. Finally, I thank the hundreds of survivors of all kinds of abuse and trauma whom I have counseled over the years for sharing your story with me, and allowing me to accompany you on your journey of healing. You taught me so much about courage and soul and Spirit. I have received much more from each of you than I was ever able to give. Your witness and strength of soul and spirit is the inspiration for this book.

—Patrick Fleming

A Note from the Publisher

We made the decision to turn the title of *Shattered Soul?* into a question because we know that readers who open these pages are questioning many things, especially whether or not the soul is permanently damaged after experiences of abuse and trauma. I have usually thought that titles shouldn't be questions, but there are things that words alone can not say well enough.

We initially selected the title *Shattered Soul*, no question mark. While working on the project *Shattered Soul*, the authors and I—as well as Paula D'Arcy who contributed the foreword to the book—had questions about making the title sound static and unquestioning.

Survivors of abuse often experience more than just wounds to their bodies and minds. Abuse and trauma can insert question marks in the most surprising of places deep within a person. The things that once seemed most sure can seem shaky and unsteady. A person's view of God and view of his or her own soul can become greatly distorted, far from a healthy perspective.

The truth that those of us involved with this project believe is that the soul itself is not shattered. It can be made whole again. It remains deep within a person, even if he or she is the survivor of unimaginable experiences.

So, we inserted a question mark where it might not seem to belong. We inserted a question mark, to make absolutely sure that survivors never insert a decisive period where it does not belong.

It is my hope that readers will rediscover something deep within themselves while reading the words of Patrick Fleming, Sue Lauber-Fleming, and Vicki Schmidt. With wisdom and compassion, the authors guide us back to wholeness.

No, your soul is not shattered.

—Marti Williams, Publisher of WordStream Publishing

Foreword

I was anxious as I arrived for my first visit to a women's halfway house in Houston, Texas, many years ago. The residents were there for six months of job training, schooling, and career guidance. Many of them had served prison time; all of them had backgrounds of abuse. I sincerely wanted to be of help, but I had no idea how to gain their trust.

When I was introduced, the room was uncomfortably silent. Each of the women was marked by pain and longing, but they were also well defended— arms crossed, disinterested stares telling me that, to them, I was yet another "do good" therapist. They were required to be in the room for this talk, but no one could force them to really listen. Clearly, I had to earn my way in.

Unable to think of what else to do, I began to share my own experience of pain and brokenness. If there is one thing I understand, it is the cry of the human heart. The deaths of my young husband and two-year-old daughter in a drunk driving accident had long ago afforded me an intimate acquaintance with dark and difficult nights that appear to hold no hope.

As soon as I started to tell my own story, the women began to pay attention. After fifteen or twenty minutes, I walked up to a young woman sitting in the front row and quietly asked if there was anything she'd like to say. In the next moment, the flood waters broke. For ninety minutes, I listened as woman after woman told a heartbreaking story. The narratives were varied, but the questions that poured from their hearts were the same:

> *Where was God when I was being abused?*
> *How do I trust again? Or find safety?*
> *Will I ever overcome this anger? Or release this shame?*
> *Is healing really possible?*

Unfortunately, the stories told in that halfway house were not unique to persons marked by prison sentences and addictions. The immeasurable suffering caused by abuse exists in all walks of life and at every level of society. Its trauma is carried by the survivor as a heavy weight capable of delivering devastating, ongoing blows. Lives that give every outward appearance of glowing success may actually conceal this private hell.

As Patrick Fleming, Sue Lauber-Fleming, and Vicki Schmidt so ably write, "Abuse traumatizes many layers of the individual." It is a hidden pain that affects every aspect of the survivor's world. The authors' commitment to changing a survivor's relationship to this pain is of immense importance.

My own life's work helps me recognize the wealth of knowledge contained in these pages. Pat, Sue, and Vicki offer not only a template for healing, but also a reason for hope. The resources they set forth are powerful tools for recovery. They liken the path to a healing pilgrimage, and the metaphor is a good one. With fierce honesty and unwavering transparency, they name the inner demons that must be faced. Then, with a conviction born of experience and love, they guide the survivor to an inner sanctuary, the waiting soul, which has remained untouched and unharmed throughout. No matter what the body and psyche endure, the soul remains unassailable. Because of this, healing is possible. Because of the soul's transcendence, the length and difficulty of the journey does not have the final say.

Interspersed among these teachings are actual journal entries of survivors. Each entry brings the text alive and acknowledges not only the deep wounds inflicted by abuse, but also the great courage of the human spirit. These personal accounts, beautifully and bravely written, add intimacy and authenticity to the considerable guidance already given. They give voice to the transformation of pain and the underlying love that holds us all.

No guide can complete the healing pilgrimage for another, but Pat, Sue, and Vicki lovingly and capably tend the fire that lights the way. Their clear guidance is respectful and comforting. They understand suffering, and they know what it is to be gripped by fear. They offer hope, not because they are optimists, but because they have seen and experienced all that is possible. Each chapter is a further affirmation that the darkness and anguish of abuse are not a match for the inner light.

Paula D'Arcy

PART ONE

Preparing for the Journey

1

Does Your Soul Feel Shattered?

It was the last counseling session of the day. My client—let's call her Becky—was describing to me the mixture of anger, sadness, and relief she had experienced a few days prior when she performed a ritual that we had devised together. To express her intense anger at God, she bought a set of cheap china dishes, placed them in a cloth bag, and brought them with a hammer to a private Catholic chapel to which she had access. After a few moments of prayer alone before the tabernacle, Becky asked God to understand and forgive what she was about to do and then laid the bag of china on the floor in front of the tabernacle. Breaking the silence of the chapel, she took the hammer and systematically shattered the china into tiny pieces to express her profound anger at the Lord.

Becky is a survivor of repeated sexual, physical, and verbal abuse, which she faced during her childhood and adolescence. I had counseled her several years previously for a considerable length of time, focusing on the psychological healing that she needed from the effects of the abuse. Although the healing was in no way complete, she had made considerable progress in the last round of counseling. When she asked to see me again, the focus of her need was different. It was now mostly about her struggle to have a fulfilling relationship with God. Becky has a deep faith. She is quite active in her parish church and in various spiritual activities with her Christian friends. She goes regularly to this chapel to pray. Her relationship with God is intense and personal, and yet very troubled.

When she returned to counseling, Becky was nearly in a rage at God about the abuse, but, at the same time, she felt guilty about her anger. She could not comprehend how a loving God could have allowed the abuse to happen to her. Our psychological work in the past had helped her to see that the abuse had not been her fault, that she had been an innocent child and teen. This had turned at least some of her anger away from herself to her abusers. Now Becky directed her anger at God. She believed in her head that God loved her, and sometimes felt it in her heart, but she did not trust God; more often, she felt strongly that a God who could have allowed such abuse could not possibly love her. In fact, her real, deeper image of the Lord was of a God who wanted to punish her for her anger and for some of the compulsive behaviors that she still struggled with as a result of the abuse. Her picture of God was the face of an abuser. Her soul was in great turmoil and distress.

You may see yourself in Becky's story. Becky's spiritual struggle, with many variations, is representative of what Sue and I have experienced with hundreds of survivors of all types of abuse for over twenty-five years now. Their abuse has not only impacted them psychologically, it has also caused them to experience a profound spiritual struggle and dislocation that we call a soul wound. You, like Becky, may be experiencing a similar wound to your soul.

Abuse of any kind, especially childhood abuse, whether sexual, physical, verbal or emotional, deeply wounds the mind and body of the victim. What sometimes has not been widely acknowledged is that abuse profoundly wounds the survivor's soul as well. Over the years, we have observed the soul damage caused by abuse. Although the psychological work that we have done with our clients has been crucial to their well-being and recovery, it has often been insufficient for bringing their full healing, peace, and joy. The soul wounds of abuse survivors have to be healed as well. Our own work has been primarily with survivors of abuse; nonetheless, we have observed that survivors of other trauma wrestle with similar spiritual struggles. You may have experienced rape, violence, war, the sudden death a loved one, or another major trauma, and so you may also be wounded spiritually.

Abuse is abuse is abuse! All abuse, all trauma, is an assault on the human spirit. The soul wounds from all different types of abuse, whether sexual, physical, verbal, or emotional, are universal, even if they differ in degree of severity. The focus of much of our counseling work in recent years has been on survivors and perpetrators of clerical sexual abuse, which is the topic of our previous book, *Broken Trust*. Because the abuser in this kind of abuse is a clergyman or clergywoman, the spiritual damage done to the survivors' soul is especially pronounced. However, we have found that all survivors of abuse suffer not only psychological damage, but similar soul damage as well. In truth, your soul cannot be damaged in itself; your spirit can ultimately never be broken. Even severe trauma and abuse do not actually hurt your soul, your deepest being and *True Self*. What we have seen, however, is that abuse and trauma can separate you from your experience of your soul, can rob you of your connection to your soul, can obscure your vision of your soul's light within you, and can block your hearing of its deep whispers of wisdom and guidance. All of this can cloud or even obliterate your knowledge and experience of your essential and eternal value and worth. Your soul itself cannot be weakened or broken. However, you can be robbed by abuse and trauma of your connection to your soul and many of its gifts and blessings. This is what makes your spirit feel broken. This is what needs mending and healing.

In response to this spiritual need, we have, through the years, gradually developed a process to help survivors of abuse and trauma heal spiritually as well as psychologically. It is a journey to reclaim their souls and mend their abused and traumatized spirits. Utilizing these insights from our counseling of survivors and building upon the pioneering healing insights of our first book, *Broken Trust*, we have identified five spiritual pathways for victims to travel. We invite you to travel them. Along the journey, you will heal your spirit and recover your soul, accompanied by your faith, your friends, and your God.

These Five Pathways are:
The Pathway of Courage
The Pathway of Holy Anger
The Pathway of Grief
The Pathway of Forgiveness
The Pathway of Transformation

As you read the subsequent chapters, these pathways will provide a spiritual GPS, mapping the way through the maze and dark thicket of abuse to a new place of light, freedom, purpose, and renewed spirit—a spirit unbroken, a soul reclaimed, a soul set free. As with all great spiritual quests, this is an arduous and challenging road. However, these pathways will help show the way. Every life change or healing is a quest. This book is a spiritual quest and journey—to heal the soul wounds of abuse and trauma, and also to ultimately transfigure the survivor's traumatic experience into new life, spiritual growth, and transformation. Join us, your fellow survivors and your friends, and walk these pathways together on this quest for spiritual healing.

This book, then, is intended to be a guidebook and companion for you, the traveler, as you journey to free and heal your soul, your *True Self*. You could call it a *Soul Help* book, or a *True Self* help book. Like any guidebook, there are many ways to use it as you journey. We have at times presented these pathways in a retreat format, structuring time to reflect, pray, or share with others their experience of the pathways. You, too, could use this book is as an extended retreat, gradually progressing through the pathways as needed, spending extended periods of time on the spiritual reflections and exercises suggested at the end of each section, which we call *Way Stations*, stopping places on the journey. This process could be shared with a spiritual director, pastor, or counselor open to and adept at spiritual matters. In fact, as with any difficult journey, this traveling is best done with a trusted spiritual companion or *soul friend*.

You will not be alone on this journey. Your God will go before you, and beside you, and be within you—whether or not you feel God's presence at any particular stage of the wayfaring. Patrick will be your narrator and navigator for the journey. We have also included stories and reflections from others who have made this pilgrimage to accompany you, help guide you, and illumine the way from their own experiences. These will be your travel companions. Their names are Sue, Vicki, Helen, Becky, and Mike (the last three names have been changed to assure their anonymity). You will hear their stories in Chapter Three and read their reflections as they travel with you on your healing journey. Whether or not their experiences of abuse were the same as or different from yours, you will find common, universal spiritual struggles and victories in their stories and reflections that you will be able to identify with and draw courage from.

Although this book is primarily directed to survivors of abuse and trauma, others of you who have been impacted by the abuse of a survivor you know and love will find the Five Pathways healing for your soul as well. Spouses, parents, friends, children, other family members, pastors, whole congregations, even counselors of the abused are impacted spiritually by the abuse experience of survivors. Trauma, and especially the abuse of the innocent and vulnerable, shakes the faith and souls of us all. Some of you who are close to survivors, or who frequently work with them, such as spouses or counselors, may experience what is called secondary trauma. This may cause you to feel some of the same psychological and spiritual wounds as the survivor. The pathways will aid your spiritual healing too. You may, in fact, want to walk through this healing process along with the survivor in your life.

This spiritual healing process does not replace the vital psychological healing process every survivor, including you, needs to undergo. The psychological healing process and the spiritual healing process go hand in hand. One will not happen without the other. Our usual experience as counselors is that the psychological phase of healing needs to begin first and eventually frees the survivor to enter the spiritual phase of healing later in the process. Counseling is normally essential to the psychological healing. None of the spiritual processes or experiences contained in this book are intended in any way to substitute for necessary emotional and psychological healing and treatment. At the same time, there is a dynamic interplay between the two spheres of our humanity—psyche and spirit—and progress in one dimension acts to potentiate healing in the other. There are many excellent resources for the psychological healing process, some of which are listed in the resources section in the back of this book.

It is important to describe briefly here our approach to spirituality in this book and in our work. The distinction has sometimes been made between spirituality and religion: spirituality is all that makes up your experience of the life of your soul; religion, for some at least, is the more-structured set of experiences and beliefs through which the life of the soul is expressed and hopefully nurtured. This book, then, is intended to be a book of soul, of spirituality, not a religious book. We ourselves come from a Catholic Christian background, our spirituality shaped and nurtured by its rich spiritual tradition as well as by the Judeo-Christian sacred writings of the Bible. At the same time, we are open to, and our spirituality has been greatly deepened and expanded by, the wisdom, practices, and sacred literature of many other great spiritual traditions of the East and the West.

In our counseling work, we often help our clients tap into and utilize their own spirituality and faith as a part of their healing process, always with great respect for their spiritual path and with no intent to impose our own spiritual beliefs. This is the approach we will employ in this book. We will draw from our own particular faith tradition, as well as from the great riches of other global spiritual traditions, as we help you make this healing journey from the depths of your own faith, spirituality, and soul. To paraphrase an old AA aphorism, we invite you to taste everything, take only what fits for you, and leave the rest.

Again, remember that you are not alone in this spiritual journey. Many others have gone before you and followed these paths to reclaim their souls from abuse. We will be with you in prayer and spirit as you traverse these ways. As it is written in Isaiah:

> *Comfort, give comfort to my people, says your God.*
> *Speak tenderly to Jerusalem,*
> *And tell her this that her bondage is at an end.*
> *A voice cries out:*
> *In the desert prepare the way of the Lord!*
> *Make straight in the wasteland a highway for our God!*
> *Every valley shall be filled in,*
> *Every mountain and hill shall be made low;*
> *The rugged land shall be made a plain*
> *The rough country, a broad valley.*
> *Then the glory of the Lord shall be revealed.*
> *—from Isaiah 40:1–5*

God desires comfort and healing for you. The Lord will speak tenderly to you on your way. God lays out a highway for you to make this journey. The obstacles, challenges, and rugged places will in time be laid low and smoothed out. Let's now step together onto this path of healing and begin to mend your spirit and reclaim your soul.

 ## *Way Station*

Each section of the book will have these Way Stations. They are like the delightful little roadside shrines found in some European countries, or the sacred Buddhist and Hindu shrines that dot the landscape in many parts of Asia. They are intended to be stopping places on your journey of soul recovery. They will provide a rest stop and some guidance to assist your spiritual healing through prayer, reflection, or some other spiritual practice. Pick and choose from the following possible activities that fit for you or create your own Way Station experience.

Choose your favored prayer or meditation practice to help you sit with what you have experienced in this first chapter. Centering or mindfulness meditation has been shown to be very helpful and healing for survivors of abuse, and some form of it is often taught today as a part of counseling or treatment. You can think of it as a tool to move beyond the clutter, anxiety, and agitation of your mind and your ego, what Buddhists call "monkey mind," and learn to be for a time in the stillness of your soul. Most spiritual traditions, including the contemplative traditions of Christianity, teach some version of this type of prayer. You may find it helpful to seek out more instruction or information about various meditation practices that fit best for you.

> Centering or mindfulness meditation has been shown to be very helpful and healing for survivors of abuse, and some form of it is often taught today as a part of counseling or treatment.

You will find that prayer and meditation will be a powerful aid to your healing journey. When you meditate, be mindful of and follow your breath as the focus of your meditation, or perhaps concentrate your attention on repeating a simple centering prayer to clear your mind and connect with your soul. Do not let yourself become frustrated or agitated by "distractions." They are usually part of the meditation process. Simply notice them, let them go, or allow them to drift away, and return your attention to your breathing or your prayer phrase. Notice without judgment what arises into your awareness. Simply watch and witness what arises into consciousness. Whether an emotion, an image, or a presence, allow yourself to be present to it, to enter into it and experience it as an expression of your soul. When you are finished with your meditation, write about your experience and insights in your journal.

2

The Five Pathways

A labyrinth is an ancient, recently re-discovered walking meditation. One of the earliest labyrinths was laid out on the floor of the magnificent Gothic Cathedral at Chartres in France. It lay there on the floor for many centuries, its full meaning and significance lost until our time. Now it has been emulated and re-constructed inside some churches and outside on the grounds of numerous retreat centers. It consists of a looping path that winds circuitously towards a center point. You, the labyrinth walker, are invited to follow this path slowly in silence and meditation, letting the Spirit speak to you as you wind this way and that, stopping wherever you feel so moved until you reach the center of the labyrinth. You are encouraged to pause there and pray or reflect on your experience of the labyrinth and on how it has spoken to your life and soul. A labyrinth is not a maze. Your spatial-navigational skills will not be challenged, and you are not likely to get lost or trapped. A labyrinth is, in fact, a pathway to the center, your center, your soul.

Not all those who wander are lost.

—from J. R. R. Tolkien's *Lord of the Rings*

The Five Pathways of spiritual healing we are inviting you to travel in this book are in some ways like a labyrinth. They are paths to your center, to the mending of your soul, and to the reclaiming of your spirit. The Pathways are a road map and a process that we have learned and developed over the years by helping to guide our clients through their journeys to heal, to reclaim their souls, and to recover from what feels like the *soul murder* of trauma and abuse.

There is a certain progression through the Five Pathways that you may want to follow. However, the pathways are not necessarily steps or stages that must be traveled in sequence. Rather, unlike a labyrinth, they are interweaving, overlapping, and intersecting paths through the maze and thicket of abuse to a center place of healing, renewal, and transformation of the soul wound of abuse and trauma. Some readers may follow the Five Pathways in sequence. For others, two or more may be experienced alternately, or at the same time. The paths may overlap, and a person following one path may double back and take an earlier path again for a time. Different readers, then, will likely find that they want

My Lord God, I have no idea where I am going. I do not see the road ahead of me. I cannot know for certain where it will end. Nor do I really know myself, and the fact that I think I am following your will does not mean that I am actually doing so. But I believe that the desire to please you does in fact please you. And I hope I have that desire in all that I am doing. I hope that I will never do anything apart from that desire. And I know that if I do this you will lead me by the right road, though I may know nothing about it. Therefore I will trust you always though I may seem to be lost and in the shadow of death. I will not fear, for you are ever with me, and you will never leave me to face my perils alone.

—from Thomas Merton's

Spiritual Master

to approach this guidebook of the soul in different ways. For instance, you may at first most identify with one of the later paths, say anger, and start there. Then you may jump to the Forgiveness Pathway and, finally, circle back to the other three pathways. As in many things, there is no one right way. In the words of Jesus, "The Spirit blows where it wills." The Spirit and your soul will lead you on this trek in the way that you need to travel it. There will be a dynamic, non-linear movement of the Spirit in your soul as you travel these roads in your own way. Choose the course, then, that fits your healing process. The pathways are guides. It is your journey.

The Five Pathways are meant, then, to be a map and a GPS for your healing pilgrimage to the center of the labyrinth of your True Self, where you can mend your spirit and reclaim your soul from the effects of abuse. They will help you to find and stay on the roads you need to travel. They will help you orienteer your inner landscape and re-locate your position if you find yourself lost. Each pathway will involve personal soul work, that is, certain challenges to be overcome and tasks to be accomplished. There will be, however, corresponding graces, spiritual tools, and soul experiences accompanying each pathway to help you surmount the challenges as you move through your healing process.

Now that you have a map, a spiritual GPS, and an initial itinerary for your journey, it is time to pack and get ready to begin! You can, of course, bring anything with you that you think will be useful. There are a few things, though, that we have found are vital to bring along with you. First of all, a journal in which you can record your thoughts, feelings, and spiritual experiences is a very useful, even crucial tool for most people who tackle this process. It can be like an alter ego, a friend, a place where your soul and your God speak to you in a very intimate and personal way. Make sure it is confidential and shared only with people you absolutely trust—if it is shared at all. You need to feel free to expose your deepest self in your journal.

Next, put in your bag any books of spiritual meaning and encouragement to you, such as the Bible, other sacred texts, or books by spiritual leaders who have inspired you. Do not pack too many though. Books are heavy and may keep you in your head. Pick ones that speak to your heart and soul and to the pain of your abuse.

Also, pack a couple of commitments to yourself. Decide that you will give your self enough time and enough moments of solitude for the meditation, prayer, reflection, and journaling this journey requires for it to be truly healing and freeing. Commit to do your best to be good to yourself during this time. A plan of self-care and self-nurturing of body, mind, and spirit is essential for such spiritual questing and healing.

A safe space is also essential. Create and bring along a special place of safety and sacredness that you can retreat to when you need solitude for reflection and prayer or for when you need a refuge from any pain that arises. This can be an actual place, like a meditation room that you create in your home, or a retreat center, chapel, or church that is available to you. It can be your bathtub, your shower, or a quiet nook at your office. It can be a place in nature that nurtures your spirit and feels safe to you. Some travelers simply maintain a sacred and quiet place in their mind. They visualize a beautiful and deserted beach or a secluded spot in the mountains. It does not matter where you locate your place of safety. What matters is that you create such a space that you can retreat to, real or imagined, that is sacred to you, that nurtures your soul, and that feels totally safe emotionally and spiritually.

The final item to take is a support network. Bring reminders of the people who love you. Keep pictures of them in your wallet, purse, smart phone, or laptop to remind yourself that you are not doing this alone. Share your journey with trusted family, friends, a therapist, a spiritual director, your pastor, or, if you are in a twelve-step program, your sponsor. You need what the Irish call an *anam cara*, Gaelic for soul friend, a person to whom you can reveal the deepest intimacies of your life, someone with whom you share your soul. Let your *anam cara* know what you are experiencing as you travel the pathways. Don't keep your pain, your struggles, your healing, and your triumphs locked inside. Share them with your *anam cara*, and make sure your soul friend knows that you will need their ears, their shoulders, their hands, and their prayers all along your path.

Now you are packed and ready to go. Let's step off into this journey of healing together. Again, remember that you are not traveling alone. We are with you. Your *anam cara* are with you. Most of all, your God goes before, walks beside you, and dwells within you in the depths of you soul. Each of your steps on these pathways will be honored and blessed and will lead you to the spiritual wholeness and spiritual awakening for which you and your soul have long yearned.

 Way Station

🍃 Choose your network of supportive soul friends. Talk to each of them and let them know what you are embarking upon. Thank them for their love and support and request that they be available when needed and be with you in prayer or spirit.

🍃 Create your safe place. If it is a physical space of your own, design it, furnish it, decorate it so that it is beautiful, cozy, and safe—a soul-nurturing place. If it is a visualized place, describe it in some detail in your journal so that you can go to it easily in your mind.

🍃 If a labyrinth is available to you, spend time in a walking meditation. Or, lacking a labyrinth, take a long walk in a quiet, natural setting. Begin by just noticing your breathing. Let it be as it is. Then be present to, or aware of, what you see, feel on your skin, smell, taste, and hear as you walk. When your mind drifts to some thoughts—worries, daily tasks to be done—gently smile at them, and bring your focus back to what your senses are taking in as you walk. If it helps, focus again on your breathing or on a silent, brief centering prayer (for example, "Lord, your peace," "Praise and thanks be to you," or "Lord, have mercy") as you follow the path. When you are finished with your walk, sit down for a few moments, and reflect on what you feel and have experienced.

> Begin by just noticing your breathing. Let it be as it is.

🍃 Think about beginning this journey of healing. What do you feel as you contemplate it? Excited and hopeful? Terrified and ready to go back? Whatever you feel is normal. Record your emotions in your journal. Bring them to your next meditation time. Breathe into them, release them on each exhale, relaxing any tight muscles as you do so. Go to your safe place, and hear what your soul has to tell you about these emotions.

3

Fellow Travelers

You will not be alone as you traverse these pathways to reclaim your soul. Your own soul and the God of your understanding will be present to you, although at times it may not feel so. Softly, gently, gradually, you may begin to experience a growing presence that actually has always been with you. You will also have traveling companions: anyone you have invited to be in your support network as well as those within this book. You will have five fellow pilgrims to travel with along the pathways of spiritual healing: Sue, Vicki, Mike, Becky, and Helen. They will be *anam cara* for you. Sue and Vicki will share extended reflections from their journals. Mike, Becky, and Helen will add shorter thoughts, letters, personal poems, and meditations that were a part of their spiritual healing.

Throughout the book, your fellow travelers' reflections on their own spiritual journeys will help light your path. They, along with millions of other people, have been where you are, experienced the psychological and spiritual pain and suffering resulting from abuse just as you have. They understand. You will feel at home with them as they share their own spiritual struggles and

In everyone's life, there is a great need for an anam cara, a soul friend. In this love you are understood as you are without mask or pretension...you can be as you really are. Love allows understanding to dawn, and understanding is precious. Where you are understood, you are at home. Understanding nourishes belonging. When you really feel understood, you feel free to release yourself into the trust and shelter of the other person's soul.
—from John O'Donohue's *Anam Cara: A Book of Celtic Wisdom*

triumphs along their paths to healing. Let them be among your soul friends and spiritual guides. Draw courage and comfort both from where they have been on their journeys and where their souls have brought them now.

In this section, we will introduce each of them and briefly tell the story of their traumatic experience so you will know what they have suffered and have had to overcome. Whether or not their experience is similar to yours, you will find common, universal, spiritual themes in their reflections that you will relate to and draw inspiration from. Each of these five companions has had, or is in the midst of, their own psychological healing process. They have worked hard in counseling and in other healing venues to overcome the emotional effect of abuse. However, the focus of their reflections will be on their spiritual journeys to reclaim their souls from abuse and on the process of transcending and transforming their abuse suffering into a new depth, freedom, and light in their spirit. Now let's meet your fellow travelers and hear their stories.

Sue is my wife, my best friend, and soul partner. Sue is in her mid-seventies. In her second career after raising five children, Sue went back to school and became first a hospital chaplain and then a psychotherapist in our private counseling, coaching, and consulting practice, which we call Double Rainbow. She specializes in counseling adult women who have experienced abuse of all kinds during their childhood and adolescence. In the past twenty-five years, she has counseled hundreds of women through their healing processes. In recent years, she has also counseled Catholic clergy who have sexually abused children and teens. She is the proud "granny" of ten grandchildren and two great grandchildren. Sue's first reflection follows this chapter. A more detailed version of her story and healing process can be found in our previous book, *Broken Trust: Stories of Pain, Hope, and Healing from Clerical Abuse Survivors and Abusers*.

Vicki is in her mid-fifties. She is currently the international director of a women's spiritual organization called Theresians International. She has worked with Mother Teresa in her community in India and in the United States, serving for a time as National Link of Mother Teresa's Co-Workers. She was the co-founder and founding director of an AIDS ministry in her hometown of Springfield, IL, was director of a retirement center, and has been involved in numerous other ministry and service projects in the U. S. and around the world.

When Vicki was seven, a tragic car accident took the life of her younger sister, Becca, who was five, and at the same time brought into her life a charismatic yet controlling priest who came to comfort Vicki and her family in their grief. Over many years, with a combination of warmth and charisma, manipulation, and verbal and emotional abuse, this priest gradually took control over Vicki's life. He drew her into the orbit of his life and ministry and increasingly made decisions for her about her life. The verbal and emotional abuse continued; at the same time, the priest's magnetism and inspiring words and work were emotionally seductive for Vicki. As she writes in *Broken Trust*:

The undercurrent, though, was that he had been reeling me into his control since I was eight. No one, including me, saw it happening. By my teenage years, he had created an allegiance to him that would be extremely difficult to defy and break. I would have done anything he asked me to do.

When Vicki was eighteen and working as his secretary, the priest's abuse and control of Vicki turned sexual. He began to force sex on her. He continued to verbally abuse her and threatened her if she tried to resist his sexual advances. This pattern of control and threat, and Vicki's extreme fear and shame, led to fourteen years of what Vicki now calls "indentured sexual servitude." Vicki sought counseling in her early thirties. With the aid and support of her counselor, Vicki was able to break free of the control and abuse of this priest and begin her healing journey of several years. A fuller account of Vicki's story can be found in *Broken Trust* and in her journal excerpts later in this book.

Mike, in his late fifties, has been an educator, and now a public speaker and retreat director, for over thirty years. He grew up in a family very much dominated and controlled by a rage-full and sadistic father. His father's emotional, verbal, and physical abuse of Mike as a child was particularly mean and calculated. He would punish Mike for some minor infraction by slapping him over and over in the face while demanding that Mike hold his face still so his father could hit him better. His father threatened further that if Mike would cry in response, he would get beaten harder. His father would devise ways to, in essence, torture Mike for real or imagined misbehavior, all the while berating him, putting him down, and calling him names. The father also sexually abused Mike's sister, and on a few occasions, was sexually inappropriate with Mike. Mike and the rest of his family, including his mother, lived in constant fear of this man. Understandably, Mike suffered many psychological and spiritual scars from this abusive background that has taken him many years to overcome.

Becky, whom you met in the first chapter, is in her forties and works as a secretary. She is very active in her church, belongs to a small prayer group community, and sings in her church choir, sometimes doing solos on special occasions or church holidays. Becky was first molested when she was seven years old by her family doctor during an examination alone in his office. Tragically, victims, once abused, are often then made more vulnerable to further abuse. Sadly, this was true for Becky.

Becky was thirteen when an adult family member began to force sex on her. The pattern was that this person would corner Becky somewhere alone in the house, sexually assault her, and tell her what an awful and ugly person she was and that she should be grateful to him because no other man would want her. He would then threaten to kill her or her family if she told anyone about what he was doing. Sometimes he would also physically abuse her to intimidate her further. Becky lived in constant fear and with deep shame and confusion about the abuse and about her developing body and sexuality. This sexual abuse continued with great frequency until Becky was able to break free from his control at age eighteen.

Helen was hardly in her teens when she experienced one single incident of sexual abuse. It was, however, a very traumatic and damaging incident. One day, when she was ten years old, she went over to play with a neighbor girl, also ten, at her neighbor's house. Helen and her friend were playing innocently together when her friend's father suddenly burst in and sexually assaulted both of them. The father threatened them both into keeping silent about the rape.

Helen did not tell anyone about this day until she entered into counseling as a young woman. Even years later, she constantly lived with the fear of another assault, never felt safe, and battled with anxious, disturbed sleep almost every night. She struggled with trusting anyone and held a great deal of anger inside. A deeply spiritual woman, she was involved in full-time ministry and felt that her fear, distrust, and anger not only kept her from being happy, but interfered with the ministry that she felt called to. This is what brought her into therapy and began her psychological and spiritual healing process. Helen is now in her mid-forties and continues to be very active in public ministry.

These are the stories, in basic outline, of the abuse experiences of your soul friends, Sue, Vicki, Mike, Becky, and Helen. As a victim of abuse or trauma yourself, you can imagine some of the pain, suffering, and emotional and spiritual scars that these stories contain. Although each story, yours and theirs, is unique, there is a shared wound and a fellowship in suffering that connects you to each other. Each of these five has had their own personal and particular journey towards healing and wholeness, psychological and spiritual. As the book progresses, they will share parts of their spiritual healing process, their path to spiritual freedom from the effects of their trauma. They will speak from the depths of their suffering and from the core of their heart and soul. Each healing path is unique. However, you will find that much of what they share will touch upon, illuminate, and help to guide and shape your own spiritual pilgrimage back to your soul.

Way Station

🍃 Notice what you feel reading this chapter's brief summaries of abuse and trauma. What similarities can you see with your own story? What differences? Can you see some or all of these fellow travelers as soul companions for your healing journey? Record your reactions in your journal.

🍃 As you reflect on ways in which you dealt with abuse or trauma in your life in the past, think about the role of other people in your healing journey. Have you developed a network or community of supportive people who have traveled with you to healing? Did you feel like you had to travel alone? Have you grown in the ability to trust others who are safe and want to accompany you on your healing path? If not, what blocks you from trusting more deeply? Can you see a way to remove, or let your soul remove, that block and allow safe, caring people to draw closer in support?

Journal

Periodically throughout the book, Sue and Vicki will share their stories and their own journeys through the Five Pathways to healing of mind and spirit. They, with Becky, Mike, and Helen, will be your fellow travelers on this pilgrimage. They are *anam cara* who are on the same road upon which you are now embarking. Sue, in this first entry from her journal, tells her story of abuse and how it affected her spiritually.

From Sue's Journal—
Everyone has a story, a very sacred story, because it is about you. It is to be listened to sacredly, respectfully, and held preciously. At the same time, we are not our story. We are not simply the sum of the events of our lives. We are much, much more. And yet each of our stories is sacred and does shed light on parts of who we are and what has shaped and formed us. So, I would like to share with you some of my own story. This journal is the record of some of my reflections on my healing journey, a journey very similar to yours. It is a peek into my soul. I invite you to come on in, share a comfortable cup of tea and a sweet with me, and listen to my story. Perhaps in doing so, a light will shine on your story as well.

My name is Sue Lauber–Fleming. How blessed I am to be the great grandmother of two, the grandmother of ten, and the mother of five living children. Two of my three daughters are adopted. Two of my babies were born alive and died: Billy lived 90 minutes, and Terese lived 45 minutes. For the past 19 years, I have been happily married to my husband, Patrick. I'm a registered nurse and a psycho-therapist. I have counseled many individuals and families who have experienced abuse. For years, I facilitated groups for hundreds of women who have been sexually, mentally, emotionally, physically, and verbally abused, abuse caused by someone who represented trust to them, a family member, neighbor, teacher, coach, or a member of the clergy. For the past nine years, Pat and I have co-facilitated a therapy and community building group at a supervised recovery community for Catholic priests and brothers, some of whom are no longer allowed to minister publicly due to sexually abusing minors.

When I was a little girl, four years old, my family and I lived in a tiny three-

bedroom house across the alley from our parish church. Our pastor, Monsignor, was an alcoholic. His behavior was sometimes erratic and scary. For instance, when he was drunk, he would careen his car down the alley at a high rate of speed, wildly honking, and sending my brothers and me scrambling back onto the stoop of our house. In one of these incidents, Monsignor even ran over and crushed my brothers' tricycles.

Since we rented this house from the church, Monsignor was our landlord and had a key to the house. One day, after my father went to work and my brothers went to school, my mother went downstairs to the basement to do laundry. My six-month old sister was sleeping, and I was upstairs playing. Monsignor used his key to very quietly sneak into our house. He went downstairs into the dark basement and, in a drunken rage, sexually assaulted my mother. Hearing my mother scream, I ran down the basement stairs, not knowing what was happening. What I saw no child should ever have to witness. My mother screamed for me to run back upstairs. As I ran for the steps, the pastor grabbed my little legs and molested me.

After Monsignor left, my mother told me to go upstairs and leave her alone. As I left, I could hear that she was crying. Later she came up upstairs. Without a word about what had just happened, my mother cleaned us up. Then we quietly folded laundry, and she fed me ice cream. The sweetness of the ice cream seemed to magically ease and calm my feelings. To this day, I go to sweets when I am upset or stressed. Nothing was ever said about this horrible incident. A few months later, our lease was up, and we moved away.

As I look back through my life, I can see how my abuse affected me. Emotionally, abuse equaled being seen and getting hurt. So to feel safe, I avoided being seen or noticed. I think that this was perhaps the most damaging spiritual wound from the abuse that I suffered. I hid myself in shame like Adam and Eve did in the Garden of Eden. I hid the light that God had given me under a bushel basket. The gifts or talents that I possessed I concealed and hid under a shroud of fear and shame.

I had a great deal of shame about my body, especially because my bedwetting continued until I was fifteen. I also bit my fingernails till they bled. Unconsciously, I believe that I suppressed some of my sexuality earlier in my life. I grew up with very low self-esteem. Because the abuse was so bad, I knew that I was bad. From the abuse of that day, I learned to be cautious, to not talk about reality, to not share feelings, to eat something sweet to numb my feelings, to stay busy at some task so as not to feel the pain. Still to this day, I am easily frightened when someone comes up from behind me. Most of all, I feared being, or letting anyone see, the real me that God had created me to be.

Surprisingly, I seemed to have been shielded from some of the worst spiritual effects of the abuse by some counterbalancing and healing spiritual experiences in my childhood. Our family remained friends with the two other young priests of our parish who were warm, loving, and fun. One evening we visited them at the rectory, and I well remember one of them greeting me with a big smile, picking me up, and gently holding me while my parents visited. These positive experiences of priests in some fashion balanced out what Monsignor did and kept me from fearing or hating all priests. Or even from feeling inside that God was in some way like Monsignor.

Another early spiritual experience was even more crucial in protecting me spiritually. When I was six years old in Sunday School, I was taught by a marvelous nun, Mother Leoline. As she prepared us for receiving First Holy Communion, she taught us a way to pray that is still meaningful to me today. She instructed us to put our heads down on the desk, close our eyes, and imagine in our minds a picture of our favorite chair at home—for me, a big red rocker that my mother used to rock us and sing to us, which I still have. Then, Mother Leoline said, imagine Father God in that chair, in that comfy red rocker. Picture yourself dressed up in your Sunday best clothes, and then run up to Father God, crawl onto God's lap, and feel God holding you and telling you how special you are to Him. Then she instructed us to picture a time when you felt badly or everything had gone wrong. For instance, sometimes I pictured how bad I felt when I wet the bed. Again, she said, crawl up on God's lap, feel his embrace, and notice that his love for you did not change whether you felt good or you felt bad. God's love didn't waver like my feelings. It was still strong and warm and comforting.

My grandmothers in their simple, humble ways taught me a lot about God. My dad's mom would always say that her faith was her shield and that it protected her from harm. I had a picture of the guardian angel in my room, and I believed she was with me, shielding me as my grandmother said. All of this childlike faith was my safety net of sanity. I could go inside into my inner tabernacle and be with my protectors even if they couldn't protect me physically or emotionally from horrendous spankings, the sporadic hysterical outbursts of my mother, or the attempted seductions of my uncle. I became quite gifted at dissociating, blocking out the bad, and living in the good. This was a spiritual gift that these earlier experiences graced me with. For instance, even though things were rough at home at times, I learned to focus more on the good that I experienced at school and home—and there was much good and love in both places. School, especially, was my Disney World. It was fun, wonderful, exciting, active, friendly, and safe. How I loved every moment of it. It became my sanctuary.

PART TWO

*Soul Wounds Inflicted
on Victims of Abuse
and Trauma*

4

Soul Murder—The Effects of Abuse and Trauma on Victims' Spirituality

Throughout history, the human species seems to have an intuitive understanding that there is something within us and something beyond us that transcends the physical, external, observable world around us and that we are a part of. Whether this understanding is expressed religiously in the great spiritual traditions and belief systems of East and West, or through visual art, myth, storytelling, literature, dance, music, theater, or through the pursuit of scientific truth and the origins of the universe, we humans generally feel that there is something more about us, transcendent to us, that is beyond the material and tangible. That which is transcendent within us is named many things in many different spiritual traditions: our inner spark of the divine, our Christ or our Buddha nature, our inner essence and freedom, our wisdom box, the life breath or force that animates us, the energy of the universe within, our True Self. In this book, we will most often simply call this transcendence soul.

Because this is not a theology or philosophy text, we will not try to define soul—if it can even be defined. Suffice it to say that all of the terms for soul are attempts to describe some aspects of this ineffable, essential, eternal core of light, love, and energy, deep within and all around us, that is most truly and essentially who we are. Your soul is not only who you most essentially are, your *True Self*, it is also the life force within you that seeks to move you beyond and out of the limits of your mind, your ego, and your life circumstances. The poet Clifford Bax expresses this beautifully in his poem, *The Meaning of Man*, when he writes:

> The Glory of God is man (and woman) fully alive!
> —from St. Iranaeus's *Against Heresies*

> *And this is the meaning of man,*
> *The task of the soul,*
> *The labour of worlds, and the plan*
> *That is set for the whole,*

For the spark of the spirit imprisoned within it…
Is longing to leap into flame,
To shatter the limits of life and be lost in a glory intense
and profound
As the soul with a cry goes out into music and seeks to be
one with the sound.

Your soul, this essential core of who you are and who you can become, is in itself untouchable. It cannot be broken, damaged, weakened, or altered—even by trauma or abuse. In your soul, you remain your true and essential self, no matter what is done to you or what you experience. Your sacred worth and eternal value abides despite all that life may throw at you. Your ineradicable soul's capacity to move beyond yourself and the limits of life remains within you. You may be hurt and significantly affected by abuse or trauma, yet you have not been metaphysically damaged or diminished. Your soul endures.

What we have observed, however, is that trauma, of whatever kind, can alter and sometimes almost sever your connection with your soul. Abuse and trauma can obscure your vision of your soul's inner light. They can block your ability to hear its whispers of wisdom and guidance. They can prevent you from knowing the truth of who you are and from seeing and feeling your innate value and worth. Abuse and trauma can trap your soul like a caged bird and confine, restrain, or even block its ability to set you free and lead you beyond yourself and deeper within yourself to the divine.

The psychologist and author, Arthur Shemgold, who has done extensive studies of the effects of abuse, calls this *soul murder.* Again, your soul cannot truly be killed, but your connection with and your experience of your soul can be murdered, obliterated, or at least significantly wounded by trauma and abuse. It might best be expressed this way: the divine spark, the inner light of your soul, cannot be extinguished, but its light can be obscured from your vision by a traumatic experience such as abuse. Even when we use language in this book, such as *soul wounds* or *soul murder,* in order to describe your experience of spiritual darkness or disconnection from your inner soul life, we hold the absolute belief that nothing, including abuse, can actually damage your soul or dim its radiant and powerful light.

Pioneer family therapist, Virginia Satir, captures this well in her book, *The New Peoplemaking,* when she describes the spiritual aspect of her early counseling work with the "rejects," "untreatable" patients in the back wards of a mental hospital:

> *It was as though I saw through to the inner core of each being, seeing the shining light of the spirit trapped in a thick, black cylinder of limitation and self-rejection. My effort was to enable the person to see what I saw; then, together, we could turn the dark cylinder into a large, lighted*

screen and build new possibilities.

The soul murder caused by abuse manifests itself in a set of typical spiritual wounds. The psychological wounds experienced by the victim of abuse are well-known and documented: profound shame, low self-esteem, fear, anxiety, depression, proneness to addiction, the wounded ability to trust and the consequent difficulty in close relationships, and struggles with body image, physical self-care, and sexuality. The spiritual wounds, the broken spirit or *soul wounds*, are less familiar to most people and sometimes may seem more subtle and less damaging. Our own experience is that they are often less visible than the psychological wounds, yet are very painful and damaging indeed.

The soul wounds that we have observed in the survivors that we have treated over the years can include some or all of the following. Do any of these wounds resemble your own?

- Do you have a fear and shame-based spirituality based in shoulds and perfectionism?
- Do you have a shame-based belief that you are undeserving of God's acceptance, love, or grace?
- Is your trust in God shattered?
- Do you feel abandoned and rejected by God?
- Do you have a felt belief that God's love is conditional—and also believe that you don't meet those conditions?
- Do you have a limited or distorted image of God that results in a wounded, deformed, or distant relationship with God?
- Do you find it difficult to pray or worship?
- Do you have an inability to be in the present moment due to emotional pain from the past and constant anxiety about the future?
- Have you lost your capacity for joy?
- Do you have the tendency to despair and lose hope?
- Do you have difficulty discovering meaning or purpose for your life?
- Do you have a disposition towards spiritual self-sufficiency and a corresponding struggle with needing God and with seeing and accepting grace in your life?
- Do you use religion addictively to merely escape from or numb your pain?
- Do you find it difficult to be grateful or express thanksgiving?
- Do you have a sense of helplessness and lack of direction in life based on an inability to access the power of your soul?
- Do you have a need for control based in the fear of spiritual surrender and of accepting your powerlessness over some things in your life?
- Have you lost your faith?

Becky describes some of the soul wounds she experienced from her abuse poetically:

"The Snow-White Clouds of Darkness"
Sunlight dances on a crystal lake, reflecting bare, vulnerable trees,
A bird flies to escape an unquenchable emptiness,
And snow-white, spider-web clouds sail by quietly
on frighteningly cold winds.
It's all a mirror of my soul—empty, cold, and lonely.
And I wonder if the artist is so busy painting this winter scene
That He's blinded by the clouds and has lost sight of me.
Perhaps He's forgotten.
Perhaps I'm worth forgetting.

The spiritual wounds that we have been describing all have the effect, in one way or another, and to one degree or another, of distorting your relationship with your soul, blocking its light from your spiritual sight, and inhibiting your ability to hear the whispers of your soul's wisdom. In short, your connection to your soul is limited or even lost by these spiritual effects of abuse. The journey of this book is a pilgrimage to heal these wounds and to recover your soul connection. It is a quest to reclaim your soul and heal the brokenness of your spirit.

 Way Station

 Prayerfully read through the list of soul wounds. After some reflection, write in your journal your own list of the spiritual wounds that abuse or trauma have inflicted on you. How have these wounds affected your spirituality? Your relationship with God? Your relationship with your own soul?

 What do you feel emotionally about how your abuse has impacted you spiritually? Write these feelings in the form of a letter, addressing your emotions to God as a prayer.

 The Christian spiritual writer, Beatrice Bruteau, provides a beautiful image for a type of prayer derived from Hinduism. You can also use this prayer, from *Radical Optimism*, as a visual meditation in itself:

The Hindus say that if you look at your mind and emotions as if at the surface of a lake, you will see your agitation as rough waves. But if you continue just to look at them and notice that you who are looking are not the agitated waves, then gradually those waves will subside. They will damp down, smooth out, and after awhile the surface of the lake will be calm. Once the water is calm, it also becomes transparent. Then you can look down through it, clear to the bottom. When our mind becomes clear and transparent, we can perceive what lies at its bottom, its foundation: it is the peace of God, the divine Eternity.

You can use this visual meditation in regard to any troubling thoughts about your abuse or trauma that cloud your mind. You can see your soul wounds themselves as the "agitated waves." However, you are not the waves. You are not your soul wounds. The waves of your wounds—painful as they are—are just temporary agitations on the surface of your great depth of soul. Visualize these waves gradually subsiding and a great calm settling over the water. See, then, into the depth of who you are and into the depths of God's presence within you to the divine peace and serenity that is available to you in any moment. Although this may be difficult to fully experience at first, it is a place within you where you will arrive as you travel the Five Pathways. Reflect on your experience of this meditation in your journal. You will find it helpful to return to this visual meditation at other times on your journey through the Pathways.

5

The Longest Ten Inches: The Gap between Head and Heart

It has sometimes been said that the longest ten inches in the universe is the gap between your head and your heart. Counseling clients frequently tell us that they know something helpful intellectually in their head, but they cannot move it those ten inches into their heart, which is, metaphorically at least, where we experience many of our emotions. It is as though there is a spring-loaded metal trap door lodged somewhere in our throats that blocks our heads from convincing our hearts and changing our emotions and our actions. This trap door blocks our heads and our hearts from uniting.

A great example of this occurred in my office just a few weeks ago. Just before starting his counseling session with me, a male client found out just that he had made an accidental mistake that was going to cost him about ninety dollars. He walked into my office in an absolute rage at himself. He berated himself over and over as stupid, incompetent, and irresponsible. I pointed out to him that this incident was a simple case of forgetting, the kind that all of us humans are susceptible to, and that, in the scale of things, the mistake and the cost was not that large. His response was a classic line that I have frequently heard from my clients over the years. He said that he could see this intellectually, but emotionally, he could not stop himself from shaming himself for it. The head-heart trap door was tightly shut. It took my client the whole counseling session, and two or three days afterward, to eventually both think and feel that he was not some lower caste of human being for making this small error.

This same head-heart split can be seen spiritually as well. To one degree or another, we all tend to carry one set of spiritual beliefs in our heads and a different set of often-contrasting spiritual beliefs in our hearts and guts. The intellectual beliefs of our heads certainly have an influence on shaping our faith and spirituality, yet it is often the lower level of emotionally based beliefs that are the

> Spirituality means waking up.
> —from Anthony de Mello's *Awareness*

most powerful in forming us spiritually—at least until we bring them into the light of conscious awareness and remake and transform them. This heart level of emotional beliefs is where victims experience the spiritual wounds that we described in the previous section. This is the level where our spirituality is too often actually operating. The difficulty is that we sometimes are not aware of what is happening to us spiritually at this heart-and-gut level. It is at least partially hidden from us, something like a spiritual unconscious. We have to wake up, open our eyes, "cleanse the doors of (our) perception," and see what is happening inside of us. It is vital for the healing journey that we are embarking upon that this level of hidden beliefs and wounds be brought to awareness.

Let's look at a hypothetical, but common example. Imagine that you are in church for a Sunday service. The scripture text is from the First Letter of John 4:16:

> *We have come to know and believe*
> *in the love God has for us.*
> *God is love,*
> *and he who abides in love,*
> *abides in God,*
> *and God in him.*

The preacher begins to extol the love of God for you, and what it means for faith and life to abide in God's love. Your head assents to the idea that God is love, but in the back of your mind, you may be thinking and feeling quite differently. You may wonder how God could be love if he allowed you to be abused when you were young and vulnerable. You may think that God may be love for everyone else, but wonder how that love could be for you when this or that is defective and wrong with you. Deep down you may believe at the emotional level that God's love has major conditions to it, and that God requires you to be getting an A+ in the tests life has put before you, and you, in your estimation, are getting an F, or at best a D-. You don't feel God's love for you no matter what your head and your creed, the scripture text or the words of the preacher, try to tell you about God's love.

> All we need to do is cleanse the doors of perception, and we shall see things as they are—infinite.
>
> —from William Blake's *The Marriage of Heaven and Hell*

This head/heart spiritual split happens in all of us. It is, however, especially pronounced in victims of trauma and abuse. It is from this split that many spiritual struggles, and even crises of faith, are born. Your head alone cannot heal this split. No one else's head can heal it for you either. That is why it is crucial, in the process of reclaiming your soul, to grow in felt awareness of the soul wounds inflicted by your experience of abuse or trauma and the unconscious spiritual beliefs that were created by these wounds and that block their healing.

To help our clients develop this awareness, some years ago we wrote "A Spiritual Laundry List for Adult Children from Abusive or Dysfunctional Families" based on a similar psychological laundry list anonymously composed for Al-Anon and Adult Children of Alcoholics. We called these underlying spiritual beliefs and characteristics, "The Grease, Grit & Grime" of our spiritual dirty laundry. They are another way of expressing and describing the soul wounds from abuse and the hidden spiritual beliefs that attach to these wounds. If you have survived a traumatic experience, you may notice that these beliefs and characteristics are true of your faith as well.

 A Spiritual Laundry List

For Adult Children from Dysfunctional or Abusive Families

The **Grease, Grit, & Grime:** We seem to have several spiritual characteristics in common as a result of being raised in a wounded, dysfunctional, or abusive household.

We have imaged our Higher Power, the God of our understanding, in a distorted way due to our childhood experience of our dysfunctional, addicted or abusive parent (or other significant adult).

We find it difficult to discover and experience the God of our understanding, or, at times, even perceive within us the existence of a Higher Power at all.

We have come to believe that God is not faithful, that God is as unpredictable and untrustworthy as our wounded and abusive parent, or other abuser.

We have come to believe that God's love is conditional, and that we have God's acceptance only if we are perfect.

We think that our Higher Power demands more of us than we can give or handle, just as we once felt overwhelmed by the needs of our dysfunctional families or by the trauma of our abuse.

We find it difficult or impossible to trust our Higher Power.

Our spirituality is grim and lacks hope, joy, or serenity; we find it difficult to be hopeful or trust in the gift of love available to us.

We are consumed with the past, anxious about the future, and are unable to simply be in the moment with God, with another person, God's creation.

We fear being abandoned by our Higher Power, and so resist being drawn closer to God.

We struggle with major commitments, or even becoming aware of our life-vision, purpose, and journey.

Our spirituality is based on a sense of shame and unreasonable guilt, and is dominated by "shoulds."

Our spiritual growth is impeded by self-sufficiency, and we resist the need for God, and others, since as children we could not depend on our addicted or abusive parents.

We find it difficult to be grateful.

We have become addicted to religion.

Our spirituality has become excessively centered on self, and lacks compassion or empathy for others.

 ## *Way Station*

🍃 Reflectively read though the "Spiritual Laundry List." Which ones match your own underlying, trauma-inflicted spiritual beliefs or soul wounds? Write your own personal version of your spiritual laundry list, the "grease, grit, & grime" that identifies your abuse-based spiritual characteristics.

🍃 Think of a time when you were struggling spiritually. In your journal write a brief creed, or expression of belief, that would express what you thought about God, the world, and your self at that time. Write this from your heart, not your head, using the creed to describe the underlying, even hidden spiritual beliefs that abuse has led you to ascribe to.

🍃 Again, spend some time in meditation, centering on your breath or a short prayer. See what bubbles up within you from your soul. Write about what you experience in your journal. You will find this most helpful to do after each section of the book.

6

The Spiritual Ripple Effect on Secondary Victims of Abuse and Trauma

If, as the African proverb says, it takes a village to raise a child, it is also true that when a child is abused, the whole village is abused.

We have certainly learned from the environmental movement of our time that all of creation is interconnected in a grand ecology of inter-related life. There is a spiritual ecology as well. Every action in our environment ripples out to affect us all. Even if you are not a direct victim of abuse or trauma, you will feel its impact emotionally and spiritually. Imagine a large stone, suddenly, even violently, thrown into a serene, calm body of water. Immediately, strong ripples radiate out from this event and rock the boats of everyone in the lake. Especially in today's world of instant global communication and inter-relatedness, we are all in this huge lake of a planet together. In terms of trauma and abuse, when any one person is traumatized or abused, it ripples out to us all and rocks all of our boats.

After the victims themselves, the strongest ripple is felt by those closest to the victim: the parents, siblings, spouses, children, other close family members, and friends of the survivor. Therapists and other professionals who work closely with victims, and enter deeply into their stories and into the trauma of their abuse, can also be deeply affected. All of these individuals may experience some of the same emotional symptoms and even spiritual wounds of the survivor. There is even a name for this. It is called STS, Secondary Trauma Syndrome. Secondary victims of abuse, although to a lesser degree than the primary victim, may experience such emotional reactions as increased fear and anxiety, lowered mood, or even depression, a lessened sense of personal safety, or a heightened sensitivity to certain kinds of imagery or vulnerable situations. Spiritually, the secondary victims may, along with the victims, find themselves questioning the love, goodness, or providence of God in the light of abuse so close to them. They may experience a loss of basic trust in God or their Higher Power. This may sap their basis for hope and contribute to some feelings of despair, helplessness, and vulnerability.

Let me give some personal examples, both from my experience as a therapist who has treated hundreds of survivors of abuse, and as the husband of a wife who was abused as a child. After hearing so many stories of abuse from clients, and witnessing my wife's abuse pain, I am very sensitive to and can no longer tolerate or watch scenes in movies or television where there is violence, or any sexual, physical, verbal, or emotional abuse. I cannot stand it anymore, even when people are yelling at each other. I feel too keenly the pain that is being experienced by the recipients of these acts. I know too well the damage that is being done. This has certainly limited my viewing entertainment choices, although I'm not sure that I am missing that much!

Spiritually, my experience with the pain of so many survivors of abuse has led me to have long and sometimes heated conversations with God. How can God allow abuse? How could God have created us human beings with this dual capacity for great love and great good and yet also for great harm and destruction to each other? How does this reconcile with what many spiritual traditions describe as God's infinite love? What kind of God are you, anyway? Alan Alda, the actor, captures my spiritual struggle well when, in *Things I Overhead While Talking to Myself*, he writes:

> *If you want to take absurdity by the neck and shake it till its brains rattle, you can try to find out how it is that people can see one another as less than human. How can people be capable of both nurture and torture?*

At times, my belief and my trust in God has been shaken and sorely tested by these questions about abuse. Over the years, I have found ways to work this out with God, and it is has not been, and sometimes still is not, easy.

Even those not intimately connected to a survivor of abuse or trauma can be secondary victims, and these individuals can be impacted spiritually as well. This is a further, although still powerful, spiritual ripple from abuse. For instance, this is seen when abuse affects the faith and spirituality of those not directly related to victims of abuse, but who belong to groups, communities, and organizations in which abuse has occurred. This is especially true when abuse has occurred within a church. In recent years, this has been seen most dramatically in the Catholic Church in its struggle to face and respond to the revelation of sexual abuse by some of its clergy. Both the reality of such abuse and the inability of too many of the church's leaders to react openly and healthfully has shocked many Catholics and left them spiritually stunned. Their trust in the guidance and teaching of their spiritual leaders is shaken. The morale and ministry of many healthy, spiritual, and non-abusive Catholic priests, brothers, sisters, and lay ministers has been undermined.

Trauma and abuse touch us all psychologically and spiritually. We are all shaken and challenged, a little or a lot, subtly or dramatically, consciously or unconsciously, by the spiritual questions trauma and abuse raise for us. If you are aware of this in your self, if you are a secondary victim of abuse, you will find the journey of healing in this book necessary and powerful. You may make this pilgrimage primarily to accompany the survivor you love, or you are doing it for your own sake. Either way, you will find aspects of the soul wounds that apply to you and experience your own need for healing. Welcome to the path.

 Way Station

🌿 If you are closely connected to a victim or are part of an organization or church that has been impacted by abuse of any kind, how has this affected you spiritually? What is your own need of healing?

🌿 Whether you are a primary or secondary survivor, read through the list of spiritual wounds in Chapter Three and the "Spiritual Laundry List" in Chapter Four from the perspective of a secondary victim of trauma or abuse. Which of these wounds or characteristics describe your spiritual experience?

🌿 What is your dialogue with God about abuse? In your journal, write it out as a conversation with God and your self.

PART THREE

The Pathway of Courage

7

Your Soul's Courage over Fear

Several years ago, I had a weird and frightening experience on top of a mountain. I was at a professional conference in Crested Butte, Colorado. Two other colleagues, fellow therapists, and I decided to hike to the top of Mount Crested Butte. Despite being a Mid-west boy, I have camped and hiked in the mountains since I was nineteen. It is one of my great loves in life. However, I had never climbed to the very top of a peak. This was going to be it.

It was a brilliant, blue-sky mountain day. All had gone well during the hike, and we were within a couple of hundred yards from the top of Mount Crested Butte. The climb the rest of the way was relatively easy, but the path had narrowed, and there was a sheer drop-off of thousands of feet on one side. I felt a twinge of anxiety, but told myself I was going to make it to the top. Suddenly, my vision blurred, my breathing became very rapid and shallow. I felt weak and dizzy. Then I threw myself down on the path, like I was having a seizure, flat on my back without pausing to take off my backpack. As I lay there hyperventilating, I had this absurd feeling and thought not just that I might fall off the ledge I was hiking on, but that the mountain itself was trying to throw me off! I actually dug my elbows into the dirt I was laying in to hold onto the mountain and prevent it from hurling me off!

> Fear knocked at the door; faith answered; no one was there.
>
> —Anonymous

It was then that I realized that what I was experiencing was what some of my therapy clients had described when they recounted to me their experience of a panic attack. I was having a panic attack! I had been literally seized with sudden and irrational fear. Realizing that it was only a panic attack, I began to consciously slow and deepen my breathing. I became quite bemused. Here I was, an experienced therapist, having a panic attack on the top of the mountain, believing the mountain itself was trying to throw me off! I started to laugh a bit, which eased my breathing further. I further realized that this first and only panic attack was related to an early childhood trauma that I had experienced. I felt stronger, got up, dusted myself off, turned around, and hiked back down the mountain (notice I didn't continue up to the top of the peak where my colleagues—who had left me behind, by the way—were celebrating their triumphant ascent).

Several months later, I went on a ski trip to Utah with two of my grandsons and their father. When I loaded onto the first ski lift with them, and it began to lift us higher and higher off the ground, I felt the same feeling of panic begin to grow in me. Again, I felt like I was going to fall off. I was also afraid of looking foolish or chicken if I would have a panic attack in front of my grandsons. I felt a temptation to give into the fear and get off the lift at the top, tell my family I was feeling sick, ski down to the bottom, and quit. But I decided not to let the fear control me and stop me from doing something I love so much. I was also determined not to allow my fear to keep me from enjoying the beautiful mountain winter day with my family. I kept getting back on the lift, breathing slowly and deeply, and reassuring myself that I was just fine and that the fear was irrational and unfounded. I had a great day of skiing.

This is an example, albeit about a fairly small matter, of courage overcoming fear. Courage is not the absence of fear. It is the determination to push through fear, to move forward, and to not allow fear to paralyze you or rob you of what is precious or vital to you.

> Fear is useless;
> what is needed
> is trust.
> —from Mark 5:36b

Abuse and trauma of whatever kind create great fear. The more traumatic, the greater the fear. Who or what you felt was safe was not; in fact, it became the source of your harm. Trust—the ultimate source of a sense of safety—was broken by your abuser. After your abuse, the world no longer felt like a safe place. Even now, the world may feel like a fundamentally hostile and dangerous place.

Traumatic fear is usually compounded by the vulnerability and helplessness of the victim. This is probably especially true for you if you experienced the abuse or trauma as a child or adolescent. Abuse can happen wherever and whenever there is the intersection of power, vulnerability, sickness, and secrecy. The combination of the power and sickness of the abuser, the vulnerability of the victim, and the enforced secrecy generates great fear in the victim. This fear can become all-consuming and dominate many or all aspects of the victim's life continuing into adulthood. Your predominant focus can become staying safe, at whatever cost. This colors and shapes all aspects of your life, including your spiritual life.

The tendency is to either live tight and small or controlling and angry, or some of both. Many victims withdraw into themselves behind thick high walls to keep everyone away from the vulnerable inner core of the self. One of my clients who had been repeatedly physically, sexually, and emotionally abused as a child, and who was an avid Science Fiction buff, described his life this way: he lived safely hidden and protected by a high tech fortress with walls made of ultra-strong exotic metals, manned by many mechanized creatures who were primarily gigantic rotating eyes that constantly scanned for any approaching danger in the form of people or situations that could hurt him again. It was very lonely inside of this fortress, and, despite the elaborate fortifications, he was always afraid.

Some victims respond to fear in a different way. They take the counter-attack mode. They head off vulnerability, perceived danger, or further abuse by angrily pushing away people and controlling situations. This is the best-defense-is-a-good-offense mode of living in reaction to traumatic fear. The difficulty is that these victims live offensively, hurting people, driving them away, attempting to control everything, even that which cannot be controlled. This too is a very lonely path, and the fear is no less, just better-hidden.

Traumatic fear caused by the experience of abuse or trauma is at the root of many psychological problems and conditions: anxiety disorders, Post Traumatic Stress Disorder, Dissociative Disorders, addictions of all kinds, to name just a few. Freud maintained that the source of much psychological distress was based in inner conflicts about the sexual drive. My own observation is that our relationship with fear is the primary root of most of our distress. As one of my teachers, Patrick Carnes, writes in *Recovery Zone*, "All therapy and recovery is about coming to terms with fear." Recent brain research is even demonstrating how the fear and trauma of abuse can affect the development, sensitivity, and even structure of parts of the brain to the extent that fear becomes what Carnes calls the "head chemist of the brain." Fear is the core of all addiction.

Fear can also become a spiritual illness, a sickness of the soul. This is beyond the feeling of fear or the experience of anxiety, which we all have, and which in fact can be a very healthy, self-protective emotion. Fear becomes a soul sickness when it is a way of life, when it is your basic stance in and against life. Fear freezes you into paralysis, controls you, robs you of joy, peace, serenity, and connection. Fear constructs a frozen fortress around your soul, which becomes its prison. Fear can also become a life script and a self-fulfilling prophecy.

Over many years of working with people, I have come to the realization that it is a metaphysical or spiritual principle that if you allow yourself to be controlled by fear, you will inevitably in time create exactly what you fear. For instance, if you fear abandonment because of childhood abuse, and let this fear control you, you will eventually create the circumstances that ensure abandonment in your primary relationships. If you fear failure, and are unconsciously consumed with this fear, you will create the very failure that you fear. When the raptor of fear has its talons embedded in your head and spirit, you are at its mercy, and you will construct a life in which your fear gets what it fears.

Fear and the life of your soul are antithetical to each other. Your soul is and desires freedom, openness, space, exploration, growth, connection, oneness, transcendence, and love. Fear is fearful of all of these and tries to block or restrict you from seeking them. Fear says, "danger, danger everywhere," and preaches, "safety, safety, first and above all." Soul whispers, "trust, grow, be open, risk, explore." Your soul says to you the words of Julian of Norwich, the 15th Century English mystic: "All shall be well, and all shall be well, and all manner of thing shall be well."

Fear makes living from your soul in the life of the Spirit very difficult. Your soul invites you to experience the peace and serenity of living each moment in the present—a key spiritual tool and experience. Fear from your abuse makes this challenging, constantly drawing you back to live in the pain of your abusive or traumatic past, leaving you chronically anxious or even terrified of your projections of a catastrophic future. Eckhart Tolle describes this well in *The Power of Now*:

> *This kind of psychological fear is always of something that might happen, not of something that is happening now. You are in the here and now, while your mind is in the future. This creates an anxiety gap. And if you are identified with your mind and have lost touch with the power and simplicity of the Now, that anxiety gap will be your constant companion. You can always cope with the present moment, but you cannot cope with something that is only a mind projection—you cannot cope with the future.*

Your soul asks you to learn to let go, to accept powerlessness over what you cannot control, and to accept what is in the present moment. The soul sickness of chronic abuse-based fear makes this kind of spiritual surrender impossible. Fear drives you to hold on for dear life, to grasp, to control even the uncontrollable. While understandable because of the abuse, this gives you a false sense of security at a high cost. There is no peace, no serenity in tightly holding on; in truth, it simply makes you more frightened and insecure. Fearful clinging begets more fear in a vicious circle. Soul-centered surrender yields serenity and peace, even if it initially feels very threatening to the victim.

You can experience this difference physically with a brief exercise. Take a small object into one of your hands. Squeeze it tightly with all of your might. Keep trying to hold it tighter. Do this for about three minutes. Then notice what your body feels. Feel the tension, tightness, and perhaps even pain in your muscles all the way up your arm and into your shoulder or beyond. If you keep on doing this, your muscles will fairly soon begin to lose their strength. Now slowly, gently relax your grip on the object, eventually letting it go and dropping it from your hand. Notice how your body feels now. That is the difference between the spiritual effect of fear and soulful surrender.

Your soul craves silence, quiet, and solitude from you. Whether this comes in the form of prayer, meditation, worship, music, reading, or time in nature, these sorts of experiences nurture your relationship with your soul and allow you the quiet space to hear the whisperings of your soul's comfort and wisdom. Victims of abuse often find this kind of solitude very difficult, even frightening. You may find yourself running from silence, filling up the space with noise and busyness. You may be afraid to be quietly alone for fear of feeling the pain of your abuse or your anxiety about the future. Or if you suffer from very low self-esteem, strong shame, or even hate yourself because of the abuse, you will find it difficult to be alone in your own company because you, like most people, do not want to spend time with someone you don't love. This leads you to run away from your True Self, to flee from your soul. This robs you of the quiet joy and peace of being, abiding, at your center.

The final major spiritual effect of traumatic fear is the fear of letting God deeply into your heart and life. The ultimate antidote to fear is a relationship with that which is beyond you and with that which is most deeply within you—your God and your soul. When you know and experience that you are never really alone, you can face any fear, and it will not overcome you. For some victims, however, because of trauma or abuse, even God does not seem safe. This is especially true for survivors of clerical abuse—abuse of any kind by a religious leader. Clergy are entrusted with the sacred responsibility of both guiding your spiritual journey and symbolically representing the divine. When they abdicate their responsibility, and, in their own psychological and spiritual sickness, exploit your special trust in them for their own sick needs, trust in God is also broken, images of God are fractured, and your innermost sacred space is trampled.

This can happen to any victim of abuse, whether or not the perpetrator was a spiritual leader. Since your abuser took advantage of your vulnerability and trust, trust in God itself can be shattered. You question in great anguish. How could God allow this to be done to you? Isn't God supposed to be protecting you? If God is love, how does this love comport with the evil of abuse that has caused you so much pain? If such harm can be done to such vulnerable and innocent children, where is God? Since, then, abuse often destroys trust in God, you, like many survivors, may fear letting God come close even though your soul cries out for this closeness. As the psalmist in the Bible sings in 42:2-4:

> As the deer longs for the running waters, so my soul longs for you, O Lord. Athirst is my soul for God, the living God. When shall I go and behold the face of God? My tears are my food day and night, as they say to me day after day, where is your God?

Your soul's triumph over fear, and the healing of all of these spiritual wounds caused by traumatic fear, is the gift or grace of courage. One day, fairly early in our relationship, Sue and I were taking a drive along country roads outside of St. Louis. We were talking intensely about the many uncertainties and fearful choices that were confronting us at this time. We were both in that moment filled with and paralyzed by our fears. We turned a corner of the winding road, and suddenly came to an intersection with a new road, designated County Road FF.

We sat there for a moment silently contemplating this sign. One of us, I think it was probably Sue, said, "That road sign stands for Fuck Fear. Let's turn onto it" (pardon the language here, but no other words fit so well or capture the force of our experience—besides, that's what we said!). So we did. FF became a code word for us, a reminder to find the courage our God had given us to push through our fears and to not allow them to control us. Courage became, for us, the choice, determination, and grace to travel the FF highway. This did not mean that we did not feel fear—for courage is not the absence of fear—but that we would not live defined and confined by fear.

You can find your own FF moment, your own FF highway! Say the words to yourself: "FF." They can be as empowering and fear-dispelling for you as they were for us. You are saying, "I renounce fear, all of its works, and all of the ways it binds me emotionally and spiritually." This does not make it all go away. You will still feel fear and its power, yet you will start to dip your toe into the more powerful current of courage and begin to move through and against your fear. Your soul applauds and rejoices!

One of the greatest acts of courage you will experience as a survivor of abuse is when you break free from the iron grip of fear, break the dark silence and secrecy of abuse, and bring the abuse into the healing light by telling your story to some trusted individuals. This takes great courage, and as many of you could testify, it is often the beginning of your healing process. Telling your story, the story of your abuse, shatters the power of fear and shame over you. It breaks the poisonous, debilitating, shaming power of secrets, and activates the spiritual process of bringing darkness into the light where God's love can heal and redeem it. Years ago, Sue and I heard this universal spiritual principle at a workshop, and we have seen it validated in the lives of so many of our clients: "Love—especially God's love—brings up everything unlike itself for the purpose of healing." Eckhart Tolle, paraphrasing St. Paul in *The Power of Now*, expresses this same principle: "Everything is shown up by being exposed to the light, and whatever is exposed to the light itself becomes light."

Whether you consciously realize it or not, when you courageously tell your story, you are working with love, with God, to activate this principle to free you from fear and move you on the road to your healing. Perhaps you have already experienced this and have found the courage to share your story with one or more people. Congratulations! If you have not yet done so, do not indict yourself. It may not be time yet. If you have already told your abuse story, you can rewrite your story as a spiritual journey, sharing the effects of abuse on your soul and what you are learning to overcome them spiritually.

As you journey forward, remember that faith sees nothing to fear, even when fear knocks at your door. Faith answers the door, and no fear is to be found there. Faith and courage work together to overcome fear. By faith, I do not mean a set of dogmas or intellectual beliefs. Faith, rather, is a relationship of trust and love with God as you name and experience the divine in your life. Your soul wants to lead you to such faith and trust. One of the most frequent phrases in the Bible is "Fear not, for I am with you."

As we have said, it is very difficult for many victims of abuse to have this faith and trust. You may have felt abandoned by God during your abuse or traumatic experience. To trust God, or to believe that God is with you in your fear or will even help you banish your fear, may seem ludicrous or even downright dangerous to you. This is understandable if you feel this way. For now, courage can mean that you are determined to eventually break through these blocks and are willing to risk beginning to seek such a relationship with God. At this point in the journey on the Pathway of Courage, that is all that is required, and that is a lot.

Becky writes of her own internal war between fear and the courage to trust in her relationship with God:

> God does not want me to have my head down, ashamed of the one I am. He sees a new me not yet revealed, who will finally be free of the chains of fear by which I have been bound for so long. He sees the scars, the imperfections, the anger and the rebellion, the hurt, the denial and the stubbornness, the tears, the fear, and the guilt. And beneath it all he sees a work of art that is so valuable that nothing can detract from its beauty. When I cry, He cries; when I laugh, He laughs; when I'm mad, He gets mad for me, not at me; and when I'm scared He sends an army of angels to protect and guide me and give me courage. It is then I can, and will fall into His outstretched arms, and allow Him to lift me to heights unknown, and lift my face to see His.

 *Way Station*

🍃 A Spiritual Courage Process:

In your journal, identify and list on one side of a sheet of paper the primary ways that fear from your trauma or abuse affects you spiritually. In the middle of the page, list steps that you can take, acts of courage, to push through the fears. On the right side of the page, use your imagination to visualize how your spirituality will be different when you take these steps and note what that will feel like. Periodically check your lists to see your progress. Affirm your self and give thanks for each act of courage, small, medium, or large.

🍃 The following is a meditation that we have found to be quite powerful for many people over the years. It is called the Meditation Walk. We are inviting you to do this meditation once or twice in each pathway, each time with the same process and yet a different theme. You can either have someone—one of your soul friends, perhaps—guide you through the meditation, or you can read it over a few times, then guide yourself. Either way works well. (A word of caution for some readers: some victims of abuse who suffer from dissociative disorders may have some difficulty with this or other meditations employed in this book. One solution is to keep your eyes open while visualizing the meditation and to stay in more of a left-brain cognitive mode).

You may want to do this and other meditations in this book in your safe place if that is a physical space for you, for instance your meditation or prayer room in your house.

To enter into this meditation, find a comfortable sitting position with your back and neck straight, your feet flat on the floor, and your eyes gently closed.

Picture the Number 21 at eye level. See it clearly and distinctly. Concentrate visually on each number as you slowly count down to 0. Eliminate all outside thoughts. Keep sending your body and mind suggestions that you are relaxed and at ease with each number. At 10, clearly see your body relaxing. Different feelings or thoughts may arise. Simply let them pass through you, and focus on the numbers. You can also enter into this meditation by focusing on your breathing instead of the numbers, if that works better for you.

At the number 0, picture yourself stepping into a beautiful beach scene. See the waves, the sand, the sun, the brilliant color and vastness of the ocean. Feel the sun and the wind on your skin. Hear the crash and whoosh of the surf.

Turn around now, and face away from the sea. Looking down, you see a backpack. In it are your fears, the fears that impinge on your soul and sap your spirit. You reluctantly pick it up and put it on your back. Notice how it feels to be carrying your fears.

You see in front of you, past the beach, a beautiful forest. There is a trail leading to it. See yourself walking along the trail into the forest. Notice the trees and branches. Appreciate the coolness and the shaded light. There are friendly animals in the forest. Stop for a moment, and talk to one of the animals. The animal is very friendly. Enjoy your conversation, and remember it. Time to go on!

You reach the edge of the forest, and see an open meadow filled with wildflowers. The trail leads you down through the meadow to a clear, flowing stream with a bridge across the water. The stream has many beautiful objects and creatures in and around it. Stop for a moment to enjoy the light sparkling on the water.

Now look up from the bridge and see a shining mountain before you. Your trail leads you over the bridge, and you begin to climb the mountain. You climb through and above the clouds, above the timberline to the top of the peak. Look around you at the glory of creation.

Then you notice a large boulder to sit on and rest. You take off your backpack and unload your fears from it. Then, from the other side of the peak, a figure appears to be with you on the boulder. This figure can be anyone that your soul imagines for you: a spiritual being, God, a lost loved one, a soul friend, some deeper part of your self, or your soul itself. This person will be your guide and confidant during this time. You can discuss whatever you want. Be sure, though, to give the person your fears and to ask for the gift of courage. Let the Spirit and your soul lead you wherever you need to go with the person and share whatever you need to share.

Spend as long as you want on the boulder. When you are ready to leave, thank and say goodbye to the person. Remember what he or she said to you. Slowly hike back down the mountain, over the bridge, through the meadow, through the forest, to the beach, and to the edge of the vast ocean.

Slowly count back from 0 to 21 and open your eyes. Be aware of what and how you feel. Make no judgments about your meditation experience. There is no right or wrong, better or best with these experiences. Write in your journal what you experienced and what the person at the top of the mountain said to you. This person or being has a special meaning to you and may change each time you go up the mountain.

Journal

This is Vicki's first journal reflection. She tells her own story of abuse and describes her journey from being paralyzed and controlled by her traumatic fear to the liberating discovery of a new spiritual courage and freedom.

From Vicki's Journal—

I have been where you are. Our stories may differ in the details, but I have felt the same shame, fear, and paralysis that you have suffered or may be now experiencing. Have hope! We can together move through all of this and be free. The following excerpts from my journal describe major parts of my healing walk. Healing is available to all of us. My prayer is that my story will be a spark to energize you for your own healing journey and a light to help illumine your way. This is my story.

An abusive sexual relationship with a Catholic priest began when I was eighteen. Father had been a trusted friend of our family since my sister, Becca, died at age 5. My mother, brothers David and Stephen, Becca, and I were in a tragic automobile accident. Father entered our lives at a most vulnerable time for all of us and in many ways became a surrogate father to my brothers and me. At a time when my parents grieved the loss of their daughter, he wove himself into the fabric of our lives in a most profound way. He was a frequent and welcome visitor in my home. In my first communion picture, I am standing proudly next to him, leaning toward him like a favored child. Abuse is sometimes sudden and shocking. Sometimes, though, as in my case, abuse builds slowly till the perpetrator is completely in control of you. The emotional abuse began after my sister died, then many years later progressed to sexual abuse at age eighteen. He had manipulated himself into my life both at home and in the workplace

(I worked for him eventually at the church) in such a profound way as to make his sexual aggression toward me acceptable behavior. He had singled me out. He had set me apart and made me feel special for many years.

Some part of me knew it was not healthy to be in a sexual relationship with him. However, a co-dependency had developed over the years of emotional abuse that felt impossible to break. As the years went on, I worked hard to hide this relationship. I was extremely fearful of anyone knowing about it and yet felt powerless to stop it by myself. In 1981, I traveled to India to work with Mother Teresa of Calcutta for several months, hoping that the experience would heal some unknown, unnamed wound inside me that kept me in allegiance to him. But it did not. Perhaps it was a seed planted during that profound time in India that later germinated and gave me the strength to reach out for help. As the years went on, it became more and more clear to me that I had to find a way out of this dark oppressively abusive relationship. I grew weary of carrying such a secret.

One evening, after a spiritual conversation with a friend, it was suggested that I seek professional help. This revelation was both shocking and frightening. In that moment, I could not even imagine telling a therapist this secret. Oddly, I had never thought of seeing a therapist, even though I was struggling in my aloneness. After this suggestion, there was a shift of consciousness. It was a new awareness that the abusive relationship with a priest was more than I could sort out for myself. And this friend did not even know of the abuse, but suspected that my spiritual journey was stymied. At that time, I was not even aware that it was abusive. The name of a therapist, who lived 100 miles away, was recommended to me. This shift of consciousness was enough to give me the courage to make a phone call, even though, at the time, I had no idea where it would lead.

In my workplace, there were two doors leading into my office. Both doors were tightly closed as I covertly dialed the number of the therapist. To my dismay, no one answered, so I left a number and waited several pensive and fearful hours for a return call. This was the first hurdle to climb, and it was the seminal moment that began the journey of healing.

After a full year of counseling sessions, it was only by letter that I could come clean and break the silence about a secret abusive emotional and sexual relationship with a priest that had imprisoned my soul for fourteen years. The fear of telling that secret was monumental. The level of stress I lived with in holding the secret had begun to chip away at my soul. I believed it was mostly my fault. I believed that I was the one who initiated it. I believed I was at an impasse, although I didn't really realize what that entailed, and it seemed only despair loomed ahead.

Constance Fitzgerald, O.C.D. in her article "Impasse and Dark Night," says,

> By impasse, I mean that there is no way out of, no way around, no rational escape from, what imprisons one, no possibilities in the situation. In a true impasse, every normal manner of acting is brought to a standstill, and ironically, impasse is experienced

not only in the problem itself but also in any solution rationally attempted. Every logical solution remains unsatisfying, at the very least. The whole life situation suffers a depletion, has the word limits written upon it. Dorothee Soelle describes it as "unavoidable suffering," an apt symbol of which is physical imprisonment, with its experience of being squeezed into a confined space. Any movement out, any next step, is canceled, and the most dangerous temptation is to give up, to quit, to surrender to cynicism and despair, in the face of the disappointment, disenchantment, hopelessness, and loss of meaning that encompass one.

It is not difficult to imagine how such attitudes affect self-image and sense of worth and turn back on the person or group to engender a sense of failure, to reinforce a realization—not always exact—that their own mistakes have contributed to the ambiguity.

Constance Fitzgerald describes my stance prior to working through the fear. Communicating the details of the abuse seemed impossible. The fear of being judged harshly about something so intimate was a colossal and oppressive barrier to every endeavor of my life. It invaded my family life, my work life, and my social life. I felt powerless to change the circumstances of my life, and I was beleaguered by my own inability to create change. Hope was not something I reflected upon during this painful process of self-disclosure. However, I would find hope as I began to move through the healing process. The obsession was accompanied by the knowledge that I desperately had to end this abusive relationship. But how? And when? And under what circumstances?

Beginning to acknowledge our fear is engaging the painful impasses that leave us feeling unable to speak our truth, to heal ourselves, and to find hope amidst the darkness. There were multiple levels of fear that I didn't anticipate, such as the initial fear of calling a therapist, the fear of telling my story to a therapist, the fear of telling a trusted friend, the fear of telling my family, and the fear of exposing the priest who abused me to the diocese. Then in the end I was fearful of anyone knowing the grim details of my abuse. You see, breaking free from the secret I had cleverly buried for so long was paramount.

Richard Rohr, an author and spiritual mentor for me, reminds us that there is a darkness that we are led into by God and by grace, and then the darkness becomes the nature of the journey itself. It seemed that every step of my healing process was a confirmation that I was being led by a power outside myself, that my willingness to say the first "yes," resulted in calling my therapist, which brokered the first grace. And then saying "yes" to each new tiny step confirmed the action of God's grace towards becoming whole. Feeling so broken at times, I have to believe the consistent push was helping me to climb what I perceived then as a very high mountain. I had always been aware of God's grace in small ways. Now, I was seeing God's grace at work in giant leaps of new faith, of stepping out into the unknown and trusting the process.

Trusting the process was seminal to my willingness to continue the difficult dialogue about the abuse. The sacred space that my therapist created during those intimate conversations of describing the abuse, of speaking those unspeakable thoughts, was monumental. By her very presence and her own spiritual integrity, she became a most trusted confidant and mentor. The space she created allowed me to be vulnerable, to speak and be affirmed, to cry, and be understood, and to be angry when I needed to be angry. She very gently and painstakingly extruded these feelings from me. In doing so, she revealed the true meaning of "the patience of Job."

My therapist said over and over to me, "Love brings up anything unlike itself for the purpose of healing." The fear had to be confronted if I was ever to begin a process of healing. God's infinite love for me would allow me to bring up the most broken parts of me for the purpose of healing it.

Courage has a new meaning to me after twenty years of emotional healing. The courage to speak long-held secrets was most likely the single most difficult experience of my life. Then, learning to integrate what I learned in an intense time of counseling initiated a life-long journey of seeking to be whole. I say that in a positive light because what I learned when I had to muster the courage to speak was a lesson that would serve me the rest of my days. I quickly learned the process of change moves from chaos to clarity and eventually leads to healing, which, in turn, leads to freedom. It is not a quick fix. The courage to take that first step ignited a desire to take the next step and the next step and the next.

Telling the story to trusted family and friends began to liberate me from the fear of holding that abominable secret. All of this took time, and occasionally I trusted someone who could not hold the story in prayer and that created division. But, indeed, I kept on trusting and creating a circle of sacred trust around me that could hold this pain and this story with me. The gift of this sacred circle has surrounded me through every healing stage of this process. Thank God there are people who love us and care deeply enough to nurture the process of growth on which we have embarked. They, too, learn from our experience, and their lives have been enriched.

I remember sitting around our family dining room table and beginning to tell the story of my abuse to my mother and father. They were completely unaware of this relationship even though for a large part of the time I was living in their home. I held the secret tightly all those years. They were shocked, hurt, angry and wholly supportive of me. In the weeks that followed, my father's anger increased. One day he stormed into the parish office ready to confront my abuser. Thankfully, the priest was not there, and my father's anger was diffused. Shortly after that episode, my father simultaneously suffered a heart attack and a stroke, which created a health crisis that would eventually lead to his death. I don't know if this health crisis was precipitated by his rage, but my gut tells me that it was related.

Facing our fear is taking a long loving look at the real. When we can articulate that fear, we can find ways to heal, to grow and to become all who God has called us to be. If I knew then what I know now, the courage to take those courageous steps would have been much easier. The fear of abandonment and the fear of more shame heaped on top of an existing shame-filled life were unremitting, but with courage and grace I overcame them.

Lyn Holley Doucet begins her book, Healing Troubled Hearts: Daily Spiritual Exercises *with a deeply revealing poem and prayer that speaks to my journey through fear:*

> God has a dream of me,
> And for me, for all eternity.
> It is a dream of healing and call,
> Of life abundant with grace.
> God fashioned me as an individual
> To live an authentic life in community,
> A life based on love.
> Events in my life,
> Within and without me,
> Have warred against this authentic self of love.
> My shadows have engulfed my gifts,
> My Spirit-fire burns low, it smolders.
> I can no longer find all the pieces of the person
> God created me to be.
> Perhaps it is all the happy fault,
> this human path, this brokenness.
> For now I seek Jesus the Healer, the Inspirer.
> I want new eyes that open themselves to the reality
> Of all that I was created to be.
> Fully human, whole, not flawless,
> Helping others, and hoping with them.
> I want to shine with God's light,
> Especially through my broken places.
> I desire to walk with freedom in God's spirit.
> I believe that God is still creating me today,
> Resurrect me, my loving God.
> Make me new again,
> Able to give and to share,
> In the abundant kingdom of the Risen One.

8

Breaking the Bondage of Shame

Shame, along with fear, is one of the most damaging and debilitating effects of abuse. Shame is the emotional belief that you are bad, defective, worthless, ugly, un-loveable, or even evil. Think of the worst word you can ascribe to yourself. That is what shame from abuse wants you to believe and feel about yourself. Abuse, whether sexual, physical, verbal, or emotional, creates this by making you feel ugly, like a non-person, an object, less than any other human being. Sometimes your abuser has said this to you directly.

The direct or implicit message is that he or she is using and mistreating you in this way because you are less than others, because you deserve this abuse. Sometimes the message is simply internalized by the young victim: if this person whom I trusted is hurting and using me this way, then I must be bad, I must somehow be wrong and defective and deserve what I am getting in this abuse. If this is being done to me, I must be of little or no value.

This kind of toxic shame is painful, and its damage goes deep. It is much more than simple low self-esteem, although it certainly creates very low self-esteem. It is different than ordinary guilt, which is a healthy feeling of your responsibility for some wrong you have done. It also needs to be distinguished from healthy shame, or feeling ashamed, which is akin to guilt and is an especially strong feeling of responsibility

> Dignity is as essential to human life as water, food, and oxygen. The stubborn retention of it, even in the face of extreme physical hardship, can hold a man's soul in his body long past the point at which the body should have surrendered it. The loss of it can carry a man off as surely as thirst, hunger, exposure, and asphyxiation, and with greater cruelty.
> —from Laura Hillenbrand's *Unbroken: A World War II Story of Survival, Resilience, and Redemption*

for serious wrong that you have done. Healthy guilt and shame say that you have done something wrong against your values; toxic shame says you are wrong simply for being who you are.

Shame caused by abuse and trauma is at the root of many psychological conditions. Shame, along with fear, is the core of many of the spiritual wounds that we looked at in Chapters Three and Four. Together, they interact to create many of the internal processes that block you spiritually. I sometimes tell my clients, while holding out my hand to demonstrate, that shame and fear are like opposite sides of the same hand ready to slap you back in your place. Fear makes you believe that the world, your life, is an essentially dangerous place, so you must hole-up in your fortress of misery. Shame makes you believe that is what you deserve.

Shame has three primary, powerful spiritual effects. First, it blocks you from knowing and experiencing the infinite value of your True Self, your essence, your soul. Second, shame blocks, inhibits, and distorts your very relationship with your soul. It is a major contributor to creating any inner disconnection from your soul that you experience as a result of abuse. Finally, shame deeply affects, and can even destroy, your relationship with your God.

If you believe and are convinced deep down that you are essentially bad, as shame from abuse tells you, you cannot comprehend, believe, or feel that in your soul, you are of immense, eternal, and ultimate value—just because you are you, just because you exist. The brilliant light of the divine spark resides in your soul. Shame obscures this from your sight by placing a dark, thick blanket over this light.

Shame cuts you off from experiencing your soul's light, wisdom, and guidance. Like the sun on a cold, cloudy winter's day, you may intellectually believe that your soul is there, but you do not experience its warmth and light. If shame possesses you because of trauma or abuse, your spiritual sight is obstructed from seeing who you truly are in your infinite soul value. Your relationship with your soul center is inhibited, suppressed, undeveloped, or completely blocked. You cannot receive or believe the value of who you are, an affirmation that your soul is trying to communicate to you. Shame causes hardening and blockage of your spiritual arteries, infarcting the life-giving flow of your soul's spiritual blood.

Shame, in our experience, is also the most powerful and insidious block for a victim seeking to find or deepen a relationship with God. If abuse has convinced you that you are bad, defective, or a piece of you-know-what, it will be impossible for you to believe that God loves you, wants to draw close to comfort and nurture you. Instead, you may believe that God's approval and acceptance is conditional—and and you don't meet those conditions. You then either feel rejected and pull away or you work desperately hard through various perfection games—work, religion, and co-dependency are the most common ones—to earn God's approbation. This never works. You can never do enough. You can never make up for how bad you believe that you are. Some of this struggle can come from an abuse-manufactured distortion of your picture of God, and a lot of it comes from a shame-distorted picture of yourself.

This three-fold spiritual effect of shame prevents you from taking in and enjoying the spiritual gifts your soul and your God want for you: joy, peace, comfort, guidance, inner security, living from a felt knowledge of your infinite value, and feeling accepted, affirmed, and loved, among many other graces. This is your birthright as an ensouled being. This is what shame robs you of.

What can be done? How can you be rid of shame and of its profoundly negative effect? This is one of the most arduous and difficult parts of the healing journey for many victims. It takes great courage and determination to fight shame. It is not an overnight— three Our Fathers, three Hail Marys, three bible quotes—process. As Jesus said, this negative spirit takes much prayer and fasting to drive out.

A good part of the difficulty is that shame from abuse, like fear from trauma, feels so real. It feels true that you are bad, no good, un-loveable, etc., etc., etc. It is an emotional belief deeply engrained in your mind, emotions, and even in your body. It becomes personal dogma, difficult to shake. When shame becomes so much a part of your self-image, it colors and filters all of your perceptions about yourself and your life. You are constantly seeing what look like confirmations about your shame in your

> To value the moment means that it is okay to value ourselves, to recognize ourselves as worth it, as deserving this richness—and we have issues, questions, and beliefs about valuing ourselves. Many of us have painful or difficult histories. Certain experiences, beliefs, and projections make us feel that we are not worth it, we are not good enough, or that we have to do one thing or another to receive or assign to ourselves any value or esteem....But all of these are just issues, obscurations, and have nothing to do with the truth.
> —from A.H. Almaas's
> *The Unfolding Now*

life situations and in peoples' reaction to you. You tend to choose to be in relationships with people who shame you through their words or their treatment of you. All of this appears to substantiate what your shame has caused you to feel about yourself. The abuse or trauma made you feel that you are bad, and now you think you have gathered the evidence to prove it! Your shame lens blinds your soul's sight so that you can't see who and what you truly are: a magnificent person of great and infinite value.

A major part of breaking free of shame is to have the courage to start to believe that any toxic shame belief is an "obscuration," a covering of the truth of who you are. Toxic shame is always a complete and shameless lie! Your abuse and your abuser have taught you and made you believe this lie about yourself. Your soul is trying to tell you the truth about how valuable you are. What is a more reliable witness of your truth—your abuse and abuser or your soul? Which will win out? Just having the courage to begin to question the validity of your shame and the courage to begin to listen to your soul will begin the process of healing your shame.

Happiness researchers, a recent field of psychological study, have shown through their research that most of what makes happy people happy is how they perceive themselves and their life situations. In my clinical experience, about 90% of being happy comes from your perceptions, only about 10% from your actual life circumstances! With work we can change our perceptions, even if we cannot change our concrete circumstances. Perceptions are simply thoughts and mental filters we come to believe are true. If you are filled with abuse-based shame, 90% of your negative beliefs and filters about yourself are false, untrue, an out and out lie.

Perhaps you have heard of an acronym for fear developed, I believe, in AA. FEAR stands for False Evidence Appearing Real. I would like to propose a parallel acronym for SHAME: Shit Happening Appears to be ME! These acronyms both highlight that what appears to be scary or shaming is often based on "false evidence" that makes us believe that what we are seeing when we fear, or when we shame ourselves, is real when it isn't real or true at all. It is false evidence, a misperception, a complete distortion, and a total falsehood. Sometimes what we fear has some basis in reality—there are scary situations and a few scary people out there. Shame, however, is never real, always a lie. Your soul desperately seeks to free you from this lie. Choose now the courage to begin to question your shame beliefs and perceptions, and start to listen to your soul.

There are several ways to better listen to your soul and to help free you from shame. Meditation, or centering prayer, is one very powerful tool for letting the soul clear you of shame. Focus on a centering tool, such as your breath or a brief prayer. Notice any negative, shame-based thoughts that arise. Don't fight them or contradict them. See them as merely wispy, cloud-like mental phenomenon of no substance. We are not our thoughts; we are not our mind. Let your thoughts pass by, and return your attention to your centering tool. Gradually, sometimes after several sittings, you will hear the whispers from your soul affirming you for who you really are, the person of great value that you are. It may come as words, an image or symbol, or it may come as a slight shift of inner feeling or sensation like a beginning serenity, light or warmth. This is your soul speaking. This is what is true and real about you.

Meditation can also help you develop an internal compassionate observer or witness within yourself who can spot the shame lies of abuse and remind you of the truth of your essential worth. Meditation helps you to stand back and look at yourself from beyond your thoughts and your emotions to see yourself from the vantage point of your soul or your God. You can cultivate this further by visualizing your soul, or a spiritual mentor, or even God, looking back at you and your shame with sadness, compassion, and anger at the lie of the shame with fond bemusement, or even with love. Your inner compassionate witness will eventually help you to distance from and gradually no longer believe or feel the shame lies of your abuse.

Some years ago, Sue, in response to the shame she saw in her survivor clients, developed a process that she named *The Circle of Value*. It deserves, and will some day hopefully get, a book of its own to explain and expand its full meaning and power. I will give you the simplified version here and demonstrate how to use it in the Way Station. The Circle of Value is based on the spiritual truth that you are a magnificent person of infinite value. That just is. That is simply so. It is so because of your True Nature, your True Self, the spark of the divine that is your soul.

The Circle of Value gives a symbolic image and a process for gradually integrating this essential truth into every cell and fiber of your being. The mental process goes like this: every time you catch yourself thinking and believing a shame-based thought about yourself, or any negative self-talk, repeat the negative phrase to yourself and then add, "And I am a magnificent person of value." Then visualize placing that negative thought inside the Circle of Value. Doing this means that this negative thought, true or not, does not add to or subtract from your essential value and worth which, again, just is. This is your soul's message.

Now here is the surprising part. It is just as important to the Circle of Value process—and to your soul—that you do the same thing with any positive thoughts that your ego attempts to use to build you up, even if they are true. It is important to realize that the ego, the false-self part of you, while well-meaning in trying to protect you, contributes to the maintenance of both your shame and your fear by artificially trying to pump up your self-esteem and your false sense of control. Neither strengths nor weaknesses, virtues or vices, add to or subtract from your infinite value, which just is, totally independent of these personal characteristics. When you think of something positive about yourself, or when you receive an affirmation from someone, take it in, enjoy it, and put it in the Circle of Value. Repeat the positive phrase to yourself and add, "And I am a magnificent person of value."

If you regularly use the Circle of Value in this fashion, over a long enough period of time, you will gradually integrate your soul's truth about your True Nature and your infinite worth. Make it your daily prayer and your special sacrament. We learn and change by repetition. In sports or physical conditioning, it takes hundreds of reps to create new muscle memory. It is the same spiritually. It takes hundreds of soul reps for your mind to develop a new memory about who you really are and accept your soul's truth about you. From our experience, "it works, if you work it!"

The final spiritual weapon in the war against the lie of shame is the powerful

CIRCLE OF VALUE

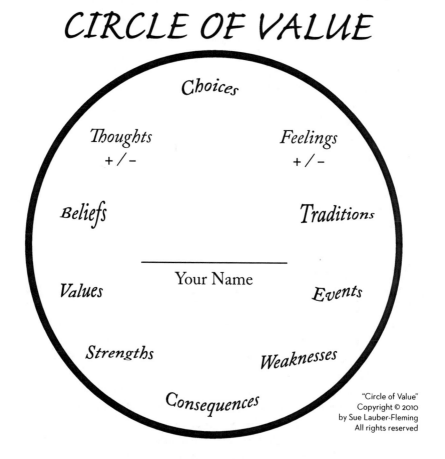

Choices

Thoughts
+ / –

Feelings
+ / –

Beliefs

Traditions

Your Name

Values

Events

Strengths

Weaknesses

Consequences

"Circle of Value"
Copyright © 2010
by Sue Lauber-Fleming
All rights reserved

And I am God's Precious Child, a Magnificent Person of Infinite Value

tool of *Acting As If.* Millions of people, especially in twelve-step recovery programs, can testify to its power. It is not just a Pollyanna approach, not just the power of positive thinking. It is based in the proven principle, based in modern brain science and physiology, that if you think and act as if something is true for long enough, whether you feel it in your emotions at first or not, it will eventually pass through those seemingly infinite ten inches between your head and heart and become real to you.

A good example is smiling. We not only smile when we are happy, we are happy when we smile. Choosing to smile, even when we feel down or sad, physiologically lifts our mood. Smiling makes us happy.

The great Buddhist teacher and living saint, Thich Nhat Hanh, captures the power of smiling and acting as if in his book, *Being Peace*, when he writes:

> *During walking meditation, during kitchen and garden work, during sitting meditation, all day long, we can practice smiling. At first you may find it difficult to smile, and we have to think about why. Smiling means that we are ourselves, that we have sovereignty over ourselves, that we are not drowned in forgetfulness. This kind of smile can be seen on the faces of Buddhas and Bodhisattvas.*

Then he offers this short meditation-poem:

> *Breathing in, I calm my body.*
> *Breathing out, I smile.*
> *Dwelling in the present moment,*
> *I know this is a wonderful moment.*

Acting As If against shame simply involves the courageous decision to believe what your soul and what your God say is the magnificent truth about you and to practice that belief on a daily basis. Ignore what your mind and your emotions, so brainwashed by your abuse and abuser, scream at you. Choose to live from the soul, to believe that you are a magnificent person of value. Act on this truth, relate from it, choose from it, pray from it, love from it, sleep in it, breath and eat from it. Regularly and mischievously smile as if only you knew and believed the magnificent secret of who you truly are. Wholeheartedly act as if it is true, and eventually your feelings will follow. You will know in your head, and feel in your heart, and it will become your secure foundation that your soul speaks the truth: you are a magnificent person of infinite and inestimable value. And your soul will rejoice in your truth and in your victory over shame.

 Way Station

Repeat the Meditation Walk as outlined in the last Way Station. This time, though, carry your shame in your backpack. When you reach the top of the mountain and your spiritual persona appears, place your shame before him or her. See and hear the response to your shame. Hear what is said about who you really are. Ask for a word, phrase, sign, symbol, or image that you can take back with you to remind you of your soul's truth about your real value and essence.

Record in your journal what you experience.

◥ The Circle of Value Exercise

Take a piece of paper, preferably a large piece of sketch pad paper

Draw a large circle filling up about three quarters of the page.

Inside the circle at the center, write your name.

Just below your name, write the words "My Soul."

Just below and outside of the circle, write the phrase "And I am God's Precious Child, Magnificent Person of Value!"

Then, several times a day for at least three months—because it takes a minimum of one hundred repetitions to begin to change an ingrained belief or habit before it begins to feel familiar and anchored in yourself—take your negative and positive thoughts about yourself, and negative or positive statements that others make about you, and write them inside the Circle of Value. Each time, repeat to yourself the negative or positive statement and then always add "And I am a magnificent person of value." For instance, you might write in the circle, and say to yourself, "I was physically abused, and I am a precious child of God, a magnificent person of value!" Each time, remind yourself that your soul and your God say that this is so and that each statement neither adds to or subtracts from your intrinsic value. Each statement about you remains and keeps you within the Circle of Value, your infinite and limitless Soul Value.

◥ Acting As If Exercise

Choose a significant stretch of time: at least a week, up to a month.

Decide with your spiritual courage that you are going to live during this time totally as if you believed in your heart that your shame was a complete lie and that your soul's message of your value was the actual and eternal truth about you.

Remind yourself every morning as you arise and every night before you go to sleep that this is how you are living during this time.

Perhaps share with your soul friend that you are doing this experiment.

Every few days, record in your journal what you are experiencing differently about yourself and your life from this new perspective, including any spiritual experiences.

At the end of the time period, reflect in your journal and with your soul friend. What has shifted and changed in you during this time? How deeply do you now believe and feel your value? What do you feel now when you hear yourself say, "And I am a magnificent Person of value"?

Journal

Fear and shame envelop the spirit of survivors like an octopus wrapping its arms around a prey. Sue, in this next entry, describes her spiritual process of breaking the grip of fear and shame in her healing journey. Her moments of courage at crucial points in her life were the key.

From Sue's Journal—

As I said earlier, abuse, for me, equated with being seen and getting hurt. Finding Courage then meant, for me, becoming visible. It meant breaking through the fear of being seen, noticed, or acknowledged: overcoming the fear to receive, the fear to even say thank you, the fear to be liked, to be listened to, to be touched gently, to be appreciated, to be seen and acknowledged as beautiful, to have my presence be enjoyed, to think for myself, to speak out loud, to know deep within that I have something worthwhile to contribute, to be heard, to share my woundedness, my weaknesses, even my successes. I feared being caught, seen as being deficient, or even being seen as excellent. I identified with "Mr. Cellophane Man" in the movie musical, Chicago, unseen and invisible, except that my fear led me to want to be that way.

One of the most life-changing acts of courage that helped to break the power of my fear and shame was when I became a cheerleader in high school. Talk about becoming visible! It scared me to death, yet something in me pushed me to try out. Something inside had to be seen. Before I went to the try-out, I stopped by my parish church. I went inside and knelt before a statue of Our Lady. Again in child-like faith, I told her and told God how much I wanted to be a cheerleader. I asked for God's help to do well in the audition. I made it! I was one of two chosen. I was not in any in-group, but I had a strong pair of lungs and an ocean of energy and enthusiasm that had been hidden deep within, waiting for this opportunity to surge forth.

I broke though my fear and became visible. My heretofore hidden talents began to emerge, a process that continued through much of my adult life. I discovered strengths and talents within me that I had never guessed were a part of me. Interestingly, priests and nuns often were the primary catalysts for my unfolding self-discovery and coming-out party: the retreat director that helped me find my voice and my gift for leadership and planning; the pastor who asked me to found a mother's club for the parish school even though, again, I was not a part of the usual social circles of the parish; a nun who encouraged me to volunteer to do pastoral care or chaplaincy ministry in her hospital, wonderful work which evolved over time into my current professional career as a psychotherapist.

God seemed to have a plan and a purpose for me. With God's help, I found the courage to make myself more and more visible, and, bit by bit, I gradually weakened the vise grip of my fear and shame. I heard an inner voice urging me to step out of the shadows. My job has been to listen and to respond with the courage to grab onto whatever rope offered me, to pull myself past my fear and into the light. Sometimes, still, when I do public speaking, or when I am the master of ceremonies for the St. Louis Strutters (a senior professional dance troupe that performs all over the country), the fear of being visible returns for a time. I think, "Do I have the right to be up in front of this audience? Do I have anything to say? Who do I think that I am?" I want to run and hide. In fact, this happens before almost all of the workshops that Pat and I present. Yet when I see the audience and begin to feel a warm connection with the people in attendance, little by little, something shifts in me. The fear evaporates, and I hear God whisper in a quiet voice inside of me: "You are my precious child. You are loved, you are good, you matter, you count, you are you, celebrate you!" Then the words begin to flow.

9

The God Problem: Transforming Your Abusive Image of God

God has a problem. To be precise, God has a PR problem, an image issue. So many people, including and especially religious people, have misused God, or their perception of God, to pursue and justify their own ego-driven agendas, sometimes even justifying violence, that God has gotten a bad name in some quarters. I love a bumper sticker I saw a few years ago: "Lord, save me from your followers!" I think sometimes that religion is like sex: wondrous, beautiful, ecstatic, and dangerous, to be deeply enjoyed and closely watched. I have fantasized sometimes that we need to set up a God Abuse Hotline where abuses and misuses of God could be reported and investigated (in my fantasy, there would also be a Bible Abuse Hotline).

God is abused also by abuse. Since God is within you, in the light of your soul, God was abused when you were abused. Part of the abuse of God is that God's image often gets distorted and deformed by the abuse in the victim's mind and heart. It is one of the most tragic effects of abuse that the victim's picture of God so often becomes damaged and, as a result, their potential for a healing and meaningful relationship with God is inhibited or blocked. Sometimes this damage to the victim's image of and relationship to God is direct. This occurs, for instance, in clerical sexual abuse, when a clergy member uses their spiritual

> Fear not, I am with you; be not dismayed; I am your God.
> —from Isaiah 41:10

position as a representative of God to manipulate their victim's special spiritual trust in order to abuse. It is also seen in what is sometimes called religious abuse, where religion is misused to shame, frighten, control, or brainwash. In these cases, the image of God is a part of the abuse and so directly distorts the victim's understanding of God.

For the majority of victims, whose abuse or trauma did not directly involve some overt misuse of religion, there still can be substantial damage to their image of God and, consequently, to their relationship with God. Trust is destroyed, shame and fear are injected, and abandonment and rejection are experienced.

Often, this gets related to or projected onto God. You come to believe that God has abandoned and rejected you as well. It becomes very difficult to trust God, to believe God is with you, loves you, and wants to draw close to you to comfort and heal your pain. In addition, abuse and trauma raise very difficult and legitimate spiritual questions that can shake your faith and spirituality. Where was God when I needed help and protection from the abuse? Why didn't God stop the abuse from happening to me? If God is love, how could he allow such an unloving act that has caused me so much pain? This is the God problem for many victims of abuse. Not all, but many victims suffer from this God problem to one degree or another.

> But Zion said, "The Lord has forsaken me, my Lord has forgotten me."
> "Can a mother forget her infant, be without tenderness for the child of her womb? Even if she shall forget, I will not forget you," says the Lord.
> —Isaiah 49:14-15

The first step in resolving the problem is to start to identify how your abuse has affected and damaged your image of God. Who is God for you? What is your picture of God? What parts of this picture have been shaped and distorted by your trauma or abuse? Does your perception of God facilitate a relationship, or does it inhibit or even block a relationship? When you go to God in prayer, meditation, or worship, what do you feel? Do you experience peace, being loved, strength, closeness, healing? Or do you feel excessive guilt, shame, fear, distance, rejection, abandonment, or nothing at all? What adjectives would best describe who God is to you: loving, close, caring, nurturing, transcendent, awesome, or distant, cold, uncaring, punishing, vengeful, rejecting, condemning? Whose face do you have on God? Is it the God of your faith, or is it the face of your abuser?

These questions will help you identify your image of God and your projections from your abuse onto God. Do not blame yourself for any negative images you discover. If you need to, blame God—God can handle it. Most of all, blame your abuse and your abuser. It is important, too, to realize that your negative, projected, abusive images of God may be hidden to you at first. Some people operate on two levels about God. There is the cognitive, faith or belief level, which may be what you profess about God and may even be primarily positive. Then there is the heart and gut level where you actually do most of your relating to and believing about God. This is where you will find your abuse has had its effect. There is an excellent exercise in the next Way Station called *The God Tree* meditation that will help you to get to the deeper levels of your God images where abuse may have wounded you.

The next step is to begin to search for new positive, life-giving images of God from which you can eventually reconstruct a new picture, free from the

effects of your abuse. There are many resources available to help you find God
anew. In the Bible, there are over forty different images of God and a host of
qualities attributed to God. Go on a Bible search for them. Other religious and
spiritual traditions offer images of God you may find appealing and life giving.
Talk to your soul friends about this. Who is God for them?

The richest resource, though, is within you: your own soul will lead and guide
you to a new vision of who God is for you. Listen to your soul quietly speaking
to you and leading you in meditation, prayer, time in nature, in dreams, in reading, in soul-searching reflection, in others' sharing. Your soul will utilize all of
these and more to help you in your search. Be awake to any new sense of that
presence of something beyond you that yields peace, serenity, joy, freedom, or
love. These experiences will help you put together a new puzzle that in time will
look like the God of your understanding.

Then one day, you will feel a new kind of presence. You will feel that your
God is truly with you, by your side, holding you in the palm of God's hand.
You will find a new peace and joy. You will feel wanted, loved, cherished, and
accepted. This will come to different people in different ways. Let your soul
surprise you. Paul Tillich, the great Christian theologian, describes one such
spiritual experience in his book, *The Shaking of the Foundations*:

> "It is though as though a voice were saying: "you are accepted, you are
> accepted, you are accepted, accepted by that which is great than you…
> Do not try to do anything now; perhaps later you will do much. Do
> not seek anything; do not perform anything; do not intend anything.
> Simply accept the fact that you are accepted!"

You will need to tap into your soul's courage to enter into this search for God.
It is always challenging to leave behind our old beliefs and venture forth for new
ones, even if the old ones made us miserable. They are familiar, secure, and paradoxically comforting. That is why letting go of them is so intimidating. We are
like a sailor hugging the shore he knows, despite being in danger of being dashed
into the rocks, because he cannot yet see the opposite shore that could give him
safety. To discover new shores, to discover new oceans, you must have the courage to lose sight of the shore. Your soul says cast off. You will be safe. There is a
better shore on the other side of your journey. There you will find a new image of
God, a divine and loving presence beyond your previous imagining.

You will particularly need courage in facing the spiritual questions that abuse
can provoke in you. These questions can shake your faith and your beliefs to the
core. They can be obstacles to your rediscovering and re-engendering a new relationship with God. The questions that I posed earlier in this section are very
common questions for survivors of trauma and abuse. Are they your questions as a
survivor? What other questions do you struggle with? It is very important to face
your questions head on at some point, even though they plunge you deep into the

heart of the mystery of suffering and God's relationship to your suffering.

It is helpful to discuss your questions with your pastor, spiritual director, soul friend, or any other spiritual guide. Pose these questions to your soul, to God, and listen. All spiritual traditions attempt to give some answer to the question of suffering, including that caused by fellow human beings. Explore these traditions and their answers. There may not be one entirely satisfying answer (which is one of the themes of the Book of Job). If you continue to search, you will eventually find an understanding of your spiritual questions about your abuse that will yield you peace and bring you even closer to God.

My own reflections on these questions, after many years of helping people to heal from their suffering, has led me to the belief that God has made himself powerless over us and our choices out of love for and respect for our freedom. Just as we are powerless over the choices and actions of the people in our lives, so God, despite great power, has willed to make himself powerless over us. Tragically, this means we are free to choose to abuse each other. At the same time, God does not want abuse to happen ever. It is never God's will. Most importantly, I believe that God is intimately present to us as we suffer, including and especially if we suffer from abuse. Though you may not feel God's presence, God is right beside you when abuse or other oppression is done to you. God is weeping with you at your pain, seething with divine anger at the injustice and at God's own powerlessness, grieving with you at the damage the abuse is causing, suffering with you in every way.

I received a visual picture for this in an autobiographical play by the well-known spiritual writer, Paula D'Arcy. Paula plays herself in this two-person play. Her friend and colleague, Tony, plays God. Paula powerfully depicts in her acting the intense suffering, despair, depression, and loss of faith that she underwent after the death of her young husband and her one-and-a-half-year-old daughter, both killed instantly by a drunk driver. What is most striking, though, is how Tony depicts God. Tony and Paula's God is never in the spotlight. He is always present to Paula, most often hovering in the background, out of the spotlight, grieving with her, next to her in her sadness, hearing her anger and despair. He never intrudes or forces anything on Paula and yet is subtly coaxing and leading her through her grief and her crisis of faith to healing and a new, deeper relationship with him. This is my picture of God's presence to us when we are struggling, suffering, or even being abused.

The experience of abuse or trauma and the questions that it produces can shake you to the very foundation of your being. It brings into question many of the beliefs and assumptions that were the spiritual bedrock of your life. Spiritual healing must then also involve a reconstruction of that fractured foundation and the discovery of new truths to live by. In a sense, you are being challenged to write a new personal creed for yourself, discarding the old understandings that no longer fit for you and incorporating the new beliefs that you discover in your spiritual healing journey. Again, your soul will be your guide.

Way Station

The God Tree Meditation

Take a moment to relax. Assume a comfortable body position. If it is comfortable for you, close your eyes; if not, leave them open. Focus on your breathing, slowly in and out. If thoughts come, notice them and gently let them go.

Imagine yourself in summer, in a beautiful natural setting, somewhere outdoors. It might be a familiar place to you or solely a place in your imagination. You are alone there, and you like being alone.

As you enjoy being in this place, you begin to sense a presence. You begin to realize that God is appearing to you as a tree! Let that tree slowly come into focus for you.

What kind of tree is your God tree? How does it look? What do you feel in the presence of the God tree? Is there something happening around the God tree? See yourself approaching the God tree. What is this like for you? What do you feel? How close can you come to the God tree?

As you are noticing the God tree, you slowly and gently become aware that you are a tree as well. What kind of tree are you? What is your tree like? Where is it in relation to the God tree? What does your tree feel like or do in the presence of the God tree? Are there any other trees near you or the God tree? What are they like?

Come out of the fantasy slowly. Let it fade from your mind's eye.

Focus again for a few moments on your breathing. Gently open your eyes and become present again to your surroundings.

Reflect in your journal on your meditation experience:

What kind of tree was your God tree? What does that mean to you? What kind of image of God might that indicate you have?

How is that image related to your abuse? What was the condition of the God tree: healthy, barren, fruitful, dead?

How close could you approach the God tree? What kind of tree were you? What was the condition of your tree? What did your tree feel like in the presence of the God tree? What does this mean about the effect your abuse has had on your relationship with God?

At some point, you can redo this meditation, visualizing this time the God you are discovering in your search for new images of God free of the abuse. What kind of tree would that be? Where is your tree in relationship to this new God tree? What kind of tree are you now? Or you may want to visualize an image of the kind of God tree you want to discover and form a relationship with, an Act As If Meditation.

🍃 Writing a New Personal Creed

Divide a large piece of paper in half lengthwise.

On one side of the paper, write in the heading "What I Now Believe."

On the other side, write the heading "What I No Longer Believe."

Reflect and pray, then list things on both sides. You do not have to list strictly religious things. Let your soul guide you however she wants to.

List the things that you now value and those that no longer fit for you.

Now look at each item on your list and be aware of the feelings that surface. Perhaps there is anger, rage, sadness, loss, hopefulness, encouragement, or surprise. These are the seeds of your spiritual healing and growth and the start of a new personal creed to build upon and live by.

Finally, when you are ready, take what you have listed on the now believe side, and write them as a personal creed. You can do this by simply filling in the blank, "I believe in _____." Do this over and over till you are complete with your creed. Post it on the wall of your prayer or meditation room.

10

Retelling Your Story as Victim, Survivor, and Thriver

We are all storytellers. Whether you are conscious of it or not, you compose, edit, tell, and re-tell a story about your life—we all do this. You have a running narrative in the back of your mind that expresses who you believe that you are, how this and that fits into your personal story, and what all of the events of your life mean in your ongoing tale. When you have a new experience or situation in your life, you work to see how it fits into your story, and this provides you with stability and security. Like everyone, you are a novelist, screenwriter, director, and the main character and star of your own life novel or movie!

This is actually a very important function of your mind. Your personal story writing gives you a sense of coherence, cohesiveness, meaning, and even purpose. Your personal narrative also profoundly shapes how you see yourself and your life. It becomes the lens through which you interpret everything that happens in your life. Because of this, your story creates many of your feelings, beliefs, and choices for

> I have had many tragedies in my life. A few of them even happened.
> —Mark Twain

your life. It actually shapes and creates your personal reality itself. For instance, if you view your personal narrative or life story through the prism of shame and despair, you will tend to create a life that reflects such a narrative. If you tell yourself the story that you are worthless, helpless, and at the mercy of others, you will live your life accordingly. If you, on the other hand, write a self-story of triumph and transcendence over great obstacles, you will likely experience and accomplish such victory in life.

Every story has a point of view, a place from which you look at, interpret, and write your personal narrative. Since you are the director of your own movie, you choose, usually unconsciously, the camera angles. Where you stand determines what you see.

I am writing this at a monastery at the foot of the Sangre de Christo Mountains of Colorado. If I look out the back window of my hermitage, I see a dry desert ravine covered with scrub bushes and trees. If I look out the front window, I view a panorama of spectacular high mountains bathed in a constant play of light and shadow. If I stay in my ravine, my view is limited. If I climb up to the top of the hill above my hermitage, a vast scene of mountains, desert, and valley, with an almost endless horizon, opens up to me.

Changing your point of view can be powerfully liberating. That is why experiences such as going on a spiritual retreat can be so life-changing and renewing. You temporarily change your point of view from your usual, busy, day-to-day camera angle. You stand in an unaccustomed place and look at your life differently. You may even see yourself from the point of view of your soul or of God.

Abuse powerfully shapes an individual's personal story, which then helps to sculpt the form of that individual's life and personal reality. As we have seen, if you are a victim, fear and shame from abuse or trauma can heavily color and define your story. However, remember that you, not your abuse or your abuser, are the author and director of your own story. You, with God, are in charge of writing and even re-writing your life script. No one else can do that for you.

> All the greatest and most important problems of life are fundamentally insolvable...they can never be solved, but only outgrown.
> —from Carl Jung's *Alchemical Studies*

As we said earlier along this pathway, at some point, you will need to tell your story of abuse. This is an act of courage that will help you break free from the silence, secrecy, shame, and fear that surround your abuse. Just telling the story is liberating and healing. If you have not yet shared your story with someone you can trust, such as a therapist, pastor, or spiritual director, it is vital that you do so.

It is also important for you to know that you can tell and re-tell your story from different points of view as your healing progresses and as you trek the different pathways of your journey. In our work with victims, we have discerned four points of view from which victims can tell and re-tell their story. All four are necessary at different phases of the healing process. The four points of view are

Victim
Survivor
Thriver
Your Soul

The first view-point is from the perspective of the victim. It is usually the first story. It is a necessary story. You are saying to yourself, the world, and your abuser:

This was done to me. You did it to me. It was not my fault.
I was and am innocent. I was vulnerable and powerless to stop the
abuse. I was a victim.

You are shedding your shame in the victim story. You are stating that what was done to you was wrong and harmful. You are putting the responsibility where it belongs, on your abuser. The victim story, though, has limitations. It can become a trap if you stay there too long. It can re-enforce a sense of helplessness and fear. It can make you believe that you do not have the inner strength to take charge of creating and shaping your life. The victim story is a narrative to eventually leave behind.

The next narrative about trauma and abuse is the story told as a survivor. This story says:

Yes, this was done to me, and it was wrong and deeply hurt me, and
yet I am still here. I'm making it. I'm getting by and even gradually
getting through what the abuse did to me. I am feeling stronger. I am
a survivor.

There is woundedness and also growing inner strength reflected in telling your abuse story from the point of view of survivor. This is a big breakthrough. Yet more is possible.

When you are ready to write the thriver story, you have progressed to the place where you can see your abuse and yourself in a profoundly different light and say to yourself and the world:

Yes, I was abused. It was wrong and hurt me. Yet the abuse no lon-
ger defines or controls me. I have risen above it, transcended it, and
have even learned how to grow stronger because of it. I am learning
to transform my abuse experience into something life-giving for myself
and others. I am thriving!

This is a powerful, transformative story about abuse that sets you completely free from the power, the shame, and the fear that your abuse had over you. We will look at this story in more depth in the fifth pathway, Transformation.

Your soul's story about your abuse can also powerfully transform your relationship to your abuse. I cannot write a script for your soul's story about your abuse. I cannot predict what that would be. Only you and your soul can discover this together. I do know that the story will be one of compassion, love, transcendence, grace, and strength from your soul. Your soul's point of view about your abuse or trauma will be completely different than the victim's story or even the survivor's story. Ask your soul to tell her story of your abuse. It will set you free and let your spirit soar far beyond the chains of your abuse. Some ideas for learning your soul's story are contained in the next Way Station.

As you can see, changing your point of view, changing your story about your abuse, can significantly shift how you feel about yourself and your life. You will experience a series of revelations as you move from victim, to survivor, to thriver, to your soul's story, as you progressively free yourself from fear and shame and discover your inner resilience, strength, power, worth, and magnificence. There is, of course, a great deal of unavoidable natural pain caused by trauma and abuse, yet the story that you tell yourself about your experiences is even more influential in how much pain you will continue to endure. The victim story can prolong and intensify your pain. The survivor and thriver stories will diminish your pain and, over time, free you from a great deal if it. Changing your point of view, re-telling your abuse story, can feel challenging and threatening. For some, it is particularly difficult to let go of the victim story. It will take courage to let go of what has become familiar to you, and move to a higher story. Again, your soul will provide you that courage and light the way.

 ## *Way Station*

If you have never written down the story of your abuse, you will find it very helpful to do it now. Write it out in your journal.

Re-read your abuse story. After some reflection, ask yourself:

Am I telling my story from the view-point of a victim, a survivor, or a thriver? Does this reflect how I now feel about myself and my life in relationship to the abuse?

Remember all three stories are necessary and good for various parts of your journey

Now, if you are ready, rewrite your story from one of the other perspectives, even if you are not quite there yet. For instance, if you have the point of view of a victim, try writing your story as a survivor. If you have the point of view of a survivor, try writing from the from the vantage point of a thriver. Notice how this feels and how it challenges and changes how you have been viewing your abuse and yourself. Come back to this exercise at various times on your healing journey and see if you are ready to again re-tell your story from another perspective.

In meditation, present your story of trauma or abuse like a movie projected on a screen. Imagine that God and your soul are your only audience. Let your spiritual imagination open you to hear and see how God and your soul respond to your abuse. How do they each see and understand your experiences? Write the new story in your journal.

An alternative way to get your soul's story of your abuse is to write a prayerful dialogue with your soul. Ask your soul how she or he views you and your abuse. How does your soul see the abuse or trauma in a different light than you have usually seen it? What questions, especially from a spiritual perspective, remain unanswered for you? Ask your soul whatever you need to ask about your abuse or trauma. Quietly, prayerfully, again with your spiritual imagination, listen for the answer. Write it down in your journal. This will become your soul's story.

You have come to the end of the Courage Pathway. Congratulations! It is time now to step onto the Anger Pathway or another pathway of your choosing. Remember, you are not alone as you journey. First, take a few moments and reflect back on your experience of this first pathway, the path of courage overcoming fear and shame, and write your thoughts in your journal.

What were the top three learnings or moments of awareness for you on this pathway?

What has changed or shifted within you on this pathway?

How can you now see and live your life differently?

On a scale of zero to ten, how strong was your fear at the start of this pathway? How strong is your fear now? Measure your shame in the same fashion. How strong is your courage now?

What do you need to commit to do for yourself to continue and build upon the positive changes you have experienced to this point?

PART FOUR

The Pathway of Holy Anger

11

God's Anger at Abuse: Restoring the Sacredness of Your Inner Temple

Anger is a powerful force and an emotion that, for many, is scary and difficult to handle well. It has the capacity to be very destructive, to be transformed into bitterness and resentment, and to corrode souls. Anger is particularly difficult for survivors of abuse because they have been victims of its destructive power. You may fear your own and others' anger. You may rarely think of anger as healing or as spiritual energy, and you certainly do not think of it as a spiritual gift or virtue. It seems inconceivable to you that anger could be holy.

Yet here in Mark's Gospel story, we have Jesus clearly angry with those who have profaned the sanctity of the temple. Furthermore, he uses his anger to cleanse the temple and drive out those who were abusing its sacredness—and not in a timid or mild way! Imagine the chaotic scene. Jesus has just come from the countryside into Jerusalem. He enters the temple area, crowded with people and bustling with activity, and sees that its sacredness has been defiled by commercialism. Filled with *just anger*, he gets physical. He overturns tables and stalls, scattering money, doves, and buyers and sellers alike. Finished with the physical part of his anger, he launches into a strong and spirited teaching, accusing those he has driven off of profaning the sacred temple, turning "the house of prayer" into "a den of thieves." No meek and mild Jesus here! Here is a man filled with just anger and indignation. This is holy anger.

In her book, *Who Are You? The Path of Self-Inquiry*, the author and spiritual teacher Gangaji says that the most important question in life is "Who am I?"

> Are you not aware that you are the temple of God, and that the Spirit of God dwells in you? If anyone destroys God's temple, God will destroy him. For the temple of God is holy, and you are that temple.
> —from *First Corinthians* 3:16-17

Jesus' actions in Mark and Paul's words in First Corinthians remind us who we are. We are all temples of God, dwelling places of the Spirit of God, body, mind, and soul. The temple of your personhood is holy, sacred, meant to be a house of prayer and Spirit. Abuse profanes and attempts to defile that sanctity. Your abuser, blinded by his or her sickness, did not respect or remember the beauty and sacredness of your personal temple, the sanctuary of your soul where God abides. Whether by sexual, physical, verbal, or emotional abuse, your sacredness was violated. The thievery here is that your abuser robbed you of the full knowledge and experience of your sacredness. You were robbed of a full connection with your True Self, your soul.

We believe that this abuse, and how it has harmed you, angers God. In and through God's anger, and in and through your own anger, God wants to restore the experience of your sacredness taken from you by abuse. God wants to help you reclaim your connection to your soul. Your own *just anger* is a part of this spiritual process of cleansing and restoration. This is the spiritual Pathway of Holy Anger.

Joining your anger to Jesus' anger, to God's anger at the abuse, is the essence of this pathway. For the survivor, at first this can be very difficult, scary, even terrorizing. Your anger feels so strong, even destructive. You have witnessed or been victimized by the destructive power of anger. You have buried, repressed, and hidden your anger for years. Your anger has been directed mainly at yourself. Or you have let your anger flare out towards others in hurtful ways. All of these ways of responding to your anger at the abuse have kept you from tapping into the potential healing in anger and blocked you from joining with God's anger. The purpose of God's anger is to cleanse and restore, not to destroy or harm yourself or others.

> When they reached Jerusalem Jesus entered the temple precincts and began to drive out those who were engaged in buying and selling. He overturned the moneychangers' tables and the stalls of the men selling doves. Then he began to teach them: "Does not scripture have it, 'My house shall be called a house of prayer for all peoples?' but you have turned it into a den of thieves."
> —from *Mark 12:15-17*

Anger has a voice which needs to be spoken and heard. If it is *just anger*— and eventually, anger tempered with mercy and love—anger's voice can be the voice of God crying out against injustice and the profaning of the temple. If you join with God's anger at the abuse, if you allow your anger to come forth, you begin to reclaim the sacredness of your personal temple, body, mind, and soul.

When you tap into your anger about the abuse and focus it on the abuser, you align your anger with God's and with God's anger you shout to the heavens:

> *I am God's precious child and a magnificent person of value. I am not bad, wrong, dirty or defective. Rather, what you the abuser did to me was wrong and sick.*
>
> *I am innocent. The abuse was not my fault. You, the abuser, are responsible for what you did to me, and for the painful wounds and suffering the abuse has caused me.*
>
> *You took advantage of my vulnerability, my innocence, and my trust to overpower me and exploit me. I now reclaim my personal power to take charge of my body, my heart, my mind, my soul.*
>
> *You made me feel worthless, desecrated, of no value. With my holy anger and God's, I drive you out and reclaim the sacredness and eternal and ultimate value of who I am and was created to be. I reclaim the holy temple of God that I am in my True Self, the sanctuary of my soul.*

You can hear and feel the soul-empowering voice of holy anger in these words from Helen:

> *Twenty-seven years ago you raped two children, your daughter and me. Evil triumphed that day in your heart, and we were its victims. I used to want you to suffer a miserable life, but now I just want to live with the satisfaction of knowing I conquered evil, I conquered you. The promise I made to stay angry, to never forget, to never forgive, perhaps served a purpose for self-preservation. At this point, I'm not sure what purpose the anger serves other than to keep you always in my life.*

In Helen's words, you witness the cleansing, healing power of her anger joined with God's. You can also sense her progression down and through the pathway of anger. First of all, Helen is able to name the abuse as evil, an evil that came from her abuser's heart, not from her own heart. Naming the evil of abuse, naming who is truly responsible for that evil, begins to turn the anger and blame away from your self as a victim, to put the responsibility where it belongs—onto the abuser. The temple is being cleansed with the scouring power of anger.

Notice that Helen, in the past, wished her abuser "to suffer a miserable life," an understandable sentiment that often comes in the early part of the journey through the anger pathway. Anger often comes with the desire for revenge or that your offender would suffer some evil or pain. However, now Helen's anger is focused on the life-giving satisfaction of knowing that she has overcome the evil of abuse and overcome the power her abuser once held over her. She has reclaimed the temple of her soul in its power and beauty.

It is clear from her words that Helen is moving toward a further progression along the anger road. She is beginning to question whether she even needs her anger any longer, whether it serves any further purpose in her healing. She is gaining the realization that anger held too long actually keeps the abuser emotionally and spiritually in your life.

Vicki expresses well the difficulty and power of freeing and expressing your anger. This is what she shared in one of our Five Pathways workshops:

> *My family did not express anger, so it was hard for me to get really pissed. I knew well into my counseling that I had to find a way to express my anger as a way to heal the shame and helplessness that I felt. My therapist would ask me to hit her couch with a whiffle bat, and I struggled to do that in her office, but at home, I could. Eventually, I found it and other physical anger outlets to be healing. Through my anger, I could finally recover my self-esteem after I placed the responsibility for its negation onto my abuser. I could finally begin to accept that I was a talented gifted woman.*

Vicki's anger freed her to take back not only her self-esteem, but also her soul-esteem, esteem for the sacredness of the temple of her soul. She could finally see and feel and live the gifts that God had placed in her. St. Irenaeus in the second century wrote, "The Glory of God is man (and woman) fully alive!" Sacred, holy anger, in union with God's anger at abuse, has the power, properly directed and channeled, to help restore you and empower you to be fully alive. That is God's greatest glory and God's greatest joy!

 ## *Way Station*

Reread Mark 12:15-17 and 1st Corinthians 3:16-17 and prayerfully reflect on their meaning in regard to your own experience of abuse:

How did your abuse take away all or some of the knowledge of your sacredness?

How strongly do you now believe and feel that you are a sacred temple of God's Spirit?

How do you feel allowing yourself to begin to be angry along with God at the abuse and the abuser, placing the responsibility for the abuse where it belongs?

How is God cleansing your personal temple from the effects of abuse and restoring your sense of your sacredness and soul esteem?

Draw, paint, or visualize your abuse happening in the courtyard of the temple as described in the Gospel. Then visualize Jesus, God, or some spiritual friend or mentor, an advocate, entering into the scene, angry at your abuser/profaner on your behalf. See your advocate confronting your abuser and driving your abuser from the temple of your life. What do you see your advocate doing? What would he or she say to your abuser? What would he or she say to you?

🖋 In your journal, write an angry letter (that you commit not to send for now) to your abuser. Then let your spirit imagine what God would add to your letter and write that into your letter as well. After you have finished both parts, read it as a part of your daily prayer for as long as needed to let it fully soak in. Read it until you can feel your own and God's just anger about your abuse.

Journal

Sue provides us now with her own experience of making her anger about her abuse a holy anger. She describes how she learned to turn her anger away from herself and focus it on the abuse still present her life. Her redirected anger became the key to discovering the sacredness of her own inner temple.

From Sue's Journal—

Early in my adult life, I was a true "rage-aholic," as my adult children can sadly testify. The rage was not so much directly from my abuse by Monsignor, but at myself for allowing abuse in various forms to continue into my adult life by being silent and not having a voice. I have come to firmly believe in what I believe is an absolute spiritual law: God's love brings up everything unlike itself for the purpose of healing. God was surfacing the anger for my healing. In time, in my early forties, I was able to transform the anger into a primal scream when I was alone in the house. I would scream not at God, or any individual, and eventually not at myself. I screamed from some very deep well of hurt and rage at all the abuse that I had allowed in my life. I would scream at the top of my lungs, turning myself inside out, refinishing my inner guts and spirit all the way down to my soul, sanding myself hard to remove all of the gunk that had accumulated inside me. This was an amazing cleansing.

My screams brought up all my fury from my past and from all the abuse that I had permitted to occur in the present. They gave voice to all that had been unsaid and kept silent out of fear because I believed that I didn't deserve to have a voice. God's love was working through my private, primal, raging screams to heal me and set me free. Gradually the screaming subsided. There was no longer a need to scream. I felt lighter. I felt alive, and, for the first time in a long time, grateful to be alive. I had room now for joy. I had space and openness to receive love and acknowledgment. I could now fully see the many blessings in my life—and they were many—and be more deeply grateful.

I was freer to let go and let God. I also had the energy to change the things in my life that were unhealthy, even abusive, and change them I did.

With God's help I live a joyous and abuse-free life today. When I get angry now, it is not from some hidden and deep tank of rage. It is anger that I can channel and harness for good. It is anger about some wrong in the present that I believe God wants to remedy. What angers me most today is when I experience being invisible to someone, but even more so when someone else is being treated invisibly or abusively or when people are making unilateral decisions for me or for other people. I am angered whenever anyone is not treated as the magnificent person of value that he or she most certainly is held to be by our God.

12

Anger as a Spiritual Antidote to the Soul Corrosion of Toxic Shame and Helplessness

Imagine that you have been forced to take a very toxic poison. Whether you were coerced, manipulated, deceived, or seduced, you have had poison ingested into your system at a time that you were very vulnerable and unable to resist. Imagine further that this is a type of poison that, although unlikely to kill you outright, is very long-lasting, insidious, and brings on a chronic toxicity and illness that effects every part of your system, even sickening your mind and your spirit. This is what the poison of trauma and abuse does to victims.

One treatment approach to a poisoning is to give an antidote to the toxin, a substance that counteracts and reverses the effects of the poison. One of the most powerful antidotes to abuse is soul-empowered anger. The word antidote is taken from the Greek word *antidoton*, which literally means, "given against." You can think, then, of your anger about the abuse as *given* to you by your soul and by your God *against* all of the poisonous effects of your abuse. It might be surprising to think of anger as given, a gift, or a grace, yet it is. It is a grace given as a counter-agent, an anti-toxin, or even an anti-venom against the shame and fear that abuse or trauma has inflicted on you.

> Hear, O Lord, a just suit; attend to my outcry; hearken to my prayer from lips without deceit. From you let my judgment come; your eyes behold what is right.
> —from *Psalms 17:1-2*

As we saw on the first pathway, courage gives you the determination to fight shame and fear. Holy anger works with courage to provide the antidote and the energy to win this fight. Anger, like sex, is a powerful life-energy that can be either life-restoring or life-destroying. The key to making your anger about your abuse life-giving is to let your soul guide you to your anger and to allow your soul to direct and channel your anger as it surfaces. This makes it holy, life-affirming anger.

Your soul's purpose for your anger is fourfold:

1) to use the energy from your anger to rediscover the sacredness and greatness of who you are and to stand in and live from that truth
2) to empower yourself to self-valuing, self-care, and healthy self-assertion
3) to rediscover and restore inner strengths that abuse hid from you
4) to gift you with the capacity to change what is wounded, unjust, or abusive in your current life situation.

This soul work of anger, then, gradually counteracts and eventually frees you from the toxic power of shame, fear, and helplessness inflicted by abuse. This is why walking the Pathway of Holy Anger for a time is so vital to your healing.

Until you are able to tap into this holy power and energy of anger, your abuse still owns you, still controls you, and defines you, sometimes decades after the abuse. Your abuser lives on in your shame and fear. When you are able to let your soul open your anger, you set yourself free from your abuse and your abuser. You place the anger where it belongs: on your abuser. You reverse the direction of your anger away from yourself where it has been so self-destructive. The energy of your anger, now soul-directed at your abuse and your abuser, breaks the hold of fear and helplessness. You can begin to be bold on your own behalf. The power of your abuser is broken, and he or she no longer lives within you.

> Sometimes our revolt expresses the Father's own revolt rather than human rebellion against him. We think we are accusing him, while in reality he is sorrowfully questioning the world through us!
> —from Pierre Wolff's *May I Hate God?*

In the Old Testament, the prophets—especially Elijah, Isaiah, Jeremiah, Hosea, Amos, and Ezekiel—stand out as heroes of holy anger. Many people mistake prophecy for prediction. The prophets were actually men spiritually gifted to see more deeply into the present moment. They learned to penetrate the surface of life with spiritual vision that enabled them to perceive the abuse and injustice around them, to see God's ways and the peoples' failure to live in those ways. These angry, zealous men would cry out from the depths of that vision to challenge the oppression and abuse of the poor and the vulnerable and call the people, especially the leaders of the faith and nation, back to God's ways of justice, truth, and healing.

When you cry out your own anger at abuse, injustice, and oppression from the depths of your soul and from your own abuse experience, then you are a prophet for yourself and for all who have been abused. In your anger, you are voicing God's own revolt, God's anger and mourning at the injustice and suffering of abuse. You are seeing more deeply the vision of who you are, how you deserved to be treated, and how you and all victims of abuse deserve now to live. This is a holy task.

When you find your own prophetic voice as a survivor of abuse by telling your story, you are applying the antidote of anger to the psychological and spiritual wounds of your abuse. You are liberating yourself and your companions in abuse from the poison of abuse that unjustly sickened you and cheated you of your soul and God-given inheritance of freedom, power, and love. No longer be afraid or ashamed of your anger. When you now find your voice and speak your anger, you are joining a great spiritual lineage, connecting you with the prophets of old, the prophets of our own time, and of many spiritual traditions who speak out in the name of Spirit and soul against abuse of all kinds.

 Way Station

Reflection Questions for your Journal:

On a scale of one to ten, how free are you to feel and express your anger about your abuse?

If this is difficult, what blocks you?

How do you express and use your anger?

Do you direct your anger at your abuser or at yourself?

Do you employ your anger to affirm yourself as an antidote to any shame that you have about the abuse?

Do you utilize your anger to empower yourself on your own behalf, asserting yourself when needed for your own welfare?

What does your soul say about your anger?

Repeat the Meditation Walk as described in the Way Station at the end of Chapter Six. This time, carry your anger about your abuse in your backpack to the mountain meeting with the spiritual being or soul mentor you encounter there. Take in what you experience in regard to your anger, and record it when the meditation is over in your journal.

After presenting your anger to your spiritual being or guide, what do you feel or experience about your anger?

What message were you given about how to direct and use your anger about your abuse?

What is your intention now about channeling your anger in life-giving and prophetic ways?

Journal

Especially if you are a survivor who has struggled with the difficult emotion of anger, you will identify with Vicki's description of her own battle with anger. Ultimately, as she relates in her story, her anger was the catalyst to breaking away from the power of her abuser and the oppression of her shame.

From Vicki's Journal—

Anger, for me, has always been a difficult emotion to express. My family dynamic did not express anger, so it did not come naturally to me. Although there were moments of disagreements or discipline by parents, we just simply did not thrive on anger or anger issues. Rarely did I hear my parents even argue about anything.

I knew well into my counseling that I had to find a way to express anger as a way to heal the shame and helplessness that I felt. Expressing anger in healthy, nondestructive ways was a cleansing process I had to learn. However, learning to express my anger would unbind my soul over time. My therapist would ask me to hit her couch with a wiffle ball bat, and I even struggled to do that in her presence. In the privacy of my own home, I could scream with rage or beat my bed with a bat. Over time I found this to be somewhat cathartic. Driving a nail into a board or engaging in physical labor became an expression of anger.

To be sure, I was angry! When I thought of somehow expressing my anger to another human, it felt deeply shameful. I carried such tremendous guilt about the relationship that being angry seemed like a contradiction, or perhaps an acknowledgement of my own culpability. The suppression of honesty or the holding of this secret over time became suppressed anger. The closer I drew to the understanding of the obscenity of the relationship that entangled me and its cost to me, the angrier I became.

At a point in the relationship, I challenged my abuser and told him that I could no longer be in a sexual relationship with him. It was then that he became incensed and began accusing me of manipulating him and causing him psychological pain. Even though he had been the sexual aggressor, he blamed me. This created a level of new anger in me that made me feel like I would explode. At this point, the veil dropped away, and the clarity of his sickness became clear. He resisted acknowledging his role in perpetrating the abuse. He would forever deny his culpability and, in fact, labeled me as psychologically unfit. He would later make this claim public and cause even deeper anger and pain for me.

As I became more in touch with all that this relationship had cost me, the anger grew to unbearable levels at times. Throughout the years of therapy, and late at night, I would begin a two-hour drive home after group therapy so enraged that I would have suicidal thoughts as I approached a bridge abutment on the highway. So many times I stared at those concrete pillars as I approached them with an intention of ramming into them and killing myself. Thank God I was never able to do that. The anger was overwhelming, and it was those peak times of feeling abandoned and hopeless that were my dark nights of the soul. One particular session in group therapy, I walked into the room in tears, and they never stopped flowing. At times I sobbed uncontrollably. The anger and hurt were intense and unrelenting. I drove home after that group meeting in much the same state of emotional distress.

Knowing the amount of pain that I harbored for such a long time, I have often been amazed at my willingness to continue on the path of healing despite such incredible anger. Anger is pain and creates more pain! I held it inside for so long, and unless I found some way to express it in a non-violent and non-threatening way, all I had left to do was to transmit it to others. I didn't want to do that. Confronting the anger felt comparable to facing a multi-headed monster.

I was angry for so many reasons: because I was used and abused; because I allowed it to happen; because it took away those precious years when I would have married and started a family of my own; because I placed so much trust in him; because the church responded in all the wrong ways; because I enabled him to be successful while my own life was being oppressed; and because I was made to feel so powerless. I held a visceral anger with the institutional church because its behavior was and, I believe, still is inconsistent with Gospel values. It doesn't have to be this way. The church's consistent denial of its own culpability in the sex abuse crisis continues to feed my interior rage. This alone has created a disconnect from the faith of my baptism. The behavior of the top leadership in my church, nationally and internationally, is inconsistent with the Gospel message of Jesus.

Eckhart Tolle says in A New Earth *that until we let go of debilitating anger and what he calls our pain-body, we cannot move forward in the spiritual life. The incapacitating anger kept me from living my true life, the life that God was calling me to live. It imprisoned me in a subservient relationship with a man whose only vision for me was in a small confined space of his own design. This ultimately affected every other relationship in my life and every other endeavor by usurping the energy that could have effectively animated my own life's journey. And, yet, amidst this, I remained deeply faithful and connected to the God who is the source and energy of my life.*

Silence and contemplative prayer played a significant role in creating a greater spaciousness to hold the anger. Mother Teresa's universal spiritual truth that "God speaks in the silence of the heart" is a profound teaching that I take to heart. I was constantly hungry for silence because I sought God's voice in all of the pain. One day, somewhat unexpectedly, I received a letter from Mother Teresa asking me to become the National Link for the Co-Workers of Mother Teresa in the United States. I happened to be volunteering at a soup kitchen in St. Louis operated by Mother Teresa's sisters. I had time after my regular therapy session and before group therapy to help with their evening meal. In a poignant moment, I felt called to sit in their chapel, in the silence of that precious space, to reflect on her request. Filled with the conflict of not knowing if I could fulfill her request, and yet realizing I could never turn down a personal request by her, I took it to contemplative prayer in that moment. I prostrated myself on the floor in front of a giant crucifix and prayed for something to arise in me that could say yes freely and with confidence. I did, of course, commit to that role, and it became a lifeline for me. It created a vision of hope amidst the deep interior pain I felt. It called me outside of myself and my own personal drama. I finally aligned myself with an energy much bigger than my personal issues. This was the key that set me free.

My friend Lyn Holley Doucet says in another place in her book, Healing Troubled Hearts, *that our wounds can keep us running from ourselves, from healing, and from God's call. Negative voices within and without drown out the simple sweet voice of the Spirit. However, the sweet voice of the Spirit is there once we can face our fear and engage our anger.*

13

Anger at God

Many victims of abuse find that they are angry with God, or even hate God, because of their abuse. At the same time, their anger often makes them feel guilty, conflicted, and afraid. They believe it is wrong, that God will punish or reject them for it, so they bury or deny their anger. If this is true of you, you are robbing yourself of a rich spiritual process and experience and blocking a further pathway of healing. Just as anger at your abuser is holy, anger at God about your abuse can be holy and healing!

However you understand or imagine God to be, whether you feel close or distant, you are in some kind of a relationship with God. Your own soul is in relationship with the sacred and the divine. In every relationship, even the most intimate and loving, there is anger. The quality of the relationship in part depends on how the anger is handled, not on the lack of anger. In my experience doing marriage counseling, I have noticed that some of the deadest and most destructive marriages are where there is buried, hidden, and unresolved anger that has turned into bitterness, or worse, indifference. Overtly angry and fighting couples, even though they need to learn how to express and channel their anger lovingly and constructively, at least show some life and energy in their relationship! It is the same with your relationship with God. If you have buried your anger about the abuse or trauma at God, your relationship will in some way be stifled, not fully alive, nor real.

If you have anger at God about your abuse and you vent it at God, lightening will not strike you. You will not be judged, rejected, or condemned. In fact, your soul will rejoice, and God will rejoice, because you are being real in the relationship and because God knows that your anger is healing for you and will eventually help to deepen the relationship between you. In fact, remember that God is also angry, not with you, but with the abuse and your abuser. When you are able to express your anger at God, you are actually joining God in his anger. God can take your anger. Who better to express it to? Your anger at God is a gift to God because you are opening your heart to God when you express it. God is present and close to you when you express your anger, not in spite of your irate words, but precisely because of them.

It is painful for parents when they hear the words "I hate you!" screamed at them by their child or teen. Every wise and loving parent, however, knows that this often is a sign that their child trusts them, loves them enough to be real with their anger, and, if listened to, will eventually turn back toward the parent and resolve the anger. If this is true of human parent-child relationships, how much more is it true of God and your self.

So if you are angry with God, be honest with yourself and with God. Name the anger or even hate, and give yourself permission to express it to God, however you feel led to do it. In the first chapter of the book, I described a very powerful and creative way that Becky employed to express her anger. Ask your soul how it would work best for you to communicate your anger at God. Your own soul encourages this as part of your healing. At first this may feel scary or shocking to do. It might cause some temporary distance in your relationship with God. In the end, it will actually bring you closer.

Genesis 32 tells the marvelous story of Jacob wrestling through a whole night with a mysterious messenger or angel of God. Jacob wrestles the angel to a draw—although the angel at the end sort of cheats—and refuses to let go of his hold on him until the angel blesses him. The angel does bless Jacob and renames him "Israel," which means "You contended with divine beings." This story is a marvelous metaphor for what happens when you allow yourself to be angry with God. You are wrestling with God. You are contending with God with the energy of your anger. You

Most religions seem to begin with the assumption that God is good. But then the believers look at the reality in front of them, and there begins the most unnerving problem: why does the just person suffer? In the Book of Job this whole problem is stretched to its limits. Job is described at the outset as a just and good man too, and yet he is not afraid to threaten and curse God for what seems like God's toleration of unjust suffering! He even puts God on trial. And God takes it, and even says Job is right! This really does show us that God is very good indeed, and humble besides. Humans can be in an actual living relationship with this kind of God.

—from Richard Rohr's *Daily Meditations*

are wrestling with God with your spiritual questions about why God could have "allowed" your abuse, or why suffering such as abuse against the innocent exists in a universe created by a supposedly loving God. Wrestling is a very intimate contact sport. You are entwined with God even as you fight.

So dare to shake your fist at God and ask why. You are in the great spiritual tradition and in the good company of people like Job and Jacob who challenged God about their suffering. You are with Jesus who cried out on the cross, "My God, my God, why have you forsaken me?" You follow in the footsteps of Buddha whose whole path to enlightenment was based on his questioning of why we suffer. Your soul invites you, then, to wrestle with God. Grapple with God about your abuse. Address your anger and your questions to God.

> Holding onto resentments is like swallowing the poison that you intended for your offender.
> —from an AA saying

Like Job discovered in his contention with God, you may not get the answers that you are looking for. However, in time you will be blessed with your own soul's resolutions of these questions, inner peace about your questions and your anger, and a deeper and more real relationship with God. You will be blessed as Jacob was. One spiritual writer, David Stendl-Rast, describes this moment when the soul and the Spirit bring peace to your questions. He says the following in his article, *Contemplative Community*:

> *In a sudden flash of insight everything makes sense; everything, life and death and the whole universe; but not as if someone had given us the solution to a complicated problem: it is rather that we are reconciled with the problem. For one moment we stop questioning and a universal answer emerges; or rather, we glimpse the fact that the answer was always quietly there, only our questions drowned it out.*

Becky, whom we first met through her holy act of breaking dishes in anger before the tabernacle in the sanctuary of her Church, is a good example of this wrestling match with God. Much of her healing journey involved expressing and eventually resolving her anger with God, as well as struggling in prayer and journaling with the faith questions her abuse assaulted her with. For instance, she writes,

> *A friend said last night that I deserve to feel good, I deserve to feel peace, I deserve to feel loved. Right now, I don't see things that way. I think I deserve to destroy something. I think I deserve to explode like I should have done decades ago. I think I deserve to scream, and kick, and punch, and gouge until all of the poison that I have been infused with is scraped*

out and not one molecule is left on the inside of me. I think that I deserve to yell at God who allowed the bad stuff to happen to me.

God, I hate you right now! I was made to be nothing more than everyone's doormat – and that includes yours! Being as old as you are, perhaps you have forgotten that I'm claustrophobic and I need my space! How am I supposed to trust you when you allowed so many bad things to happen to me? In my opinion, you're no different than my abuser who treated me like gold in front of everyone, but physically and emotionally tortured me when no one else was around.

So how would you grade me on being your child, God? Would you give me a D- since I've spent so much time being mad lately, or because I am so resistant to a lot of things, or because I'm blaming you for things you're not personally responsible for? Or would you give me an A for finally having the gumption to rid myself of all of this poison without doing anything to hurt myself or anyone else?

 ## *Way Station*

🖋 In your journal, write an angry prayer letter to God. Give yourself permission to express all of the feelings that you have about God to God in regard to your abuse.

Share your letter with a spiritual friend or a spiritual advisor.

Read and pray it daily for a week, or as long as needed, and notice what shifts in you and in your relationship with God

Take time later on to listen to any response to your letter you hear from your soul or from God. Record what you hear in your journal.

🖋 Write your spiritual questions about your abuse as a question-response dialogue with God or with your soul. Sit in meditation to quiet your mind when awaiting a response. What do you hear? What do you sense or feel in your soul? Give this process a lot of time. Come back to it off and on, and see how your questions and the responses may have changed.

🖋 Read or pray the "angry psalms": Psalms 10, 17, 22, and 142, among others. Note the freedom of the psalmist to pour out anger and other emotions at God. Reflect on how these prayer songs express or resonate with your own emotions in your relationship with God.

14

The Spiritual Dangers of the Anger Pathway

As I have been saying in the previous chapters, anger is a vital phase of the healing journey. However, your soul intends it to be only a temporary stage. It is not a place where you should stay, set up camp, or build a house of anger. It is not a path on which you should remain indefinitely. Some victims get stuck too long, even permanently, in anger at their abusers. Chronic, stuck anger will eventually become an obstacle to the healing and growth of your spirit.

Unlike a good red wine, anger does not age well. More like a cheap wine, anger held too long turns to vinegar of the spirit. Stuck anger over time becomes resentment, bitterness, depression of the mind and spirit, and even chronic hatred and aggression, passive or direct. This can become a dark pall over your spirit that obscures your vision of your soul and can, in the worst case, block your access to your soul entirely. Persistent, protracted anger is the opposite of the healing, serenity, and love that your soul desires for you; it prevents you from receiving these gifts. Anger, as we have seen, can be holy, healing, and liberating, but it can become unholy when it is obsessive, bitter, and bent on vengeance or hurt for your abuser. Wanting for a time to hurt your abuser, or for your abuser to experience pain, is an understandable expression of anger. Really desiring that hurt for your abuser as a permanent life stance is poisonous to your soul.

> If anger is the predominant energy vibration of the pain-body and you think angry thoughts, dwelling on what someone did to you or what you are going to do to him or her, then you have become unconscious, and the pain-body has become "you."
> —from Eckhart Tolle's *The Power of Now*

If you turn your heart into a weapon against your abuser, you may get some satisfaction and actually inflict some harm, but you will always end up using the hate in your heart against yourself. This is a spiritual law. Hate kills. It is a slow toxin that poisons and eats away at your spirit. As Tolle states, dwelling on and in your anger keeps you in your pain until you become the pain.

If you dwell on and in your anger, you can develop what author Patrick Carnes, in his book *The Recovery Zone*, has called a *grievance story*. You can direct your story against certain people, certain groups, or even against life, humanity, and God. Your grievance story as a victim can become one of the primary narratives about yourself and your life. It can color, shape—even distort—your whole view of your life. You can hold onto your grievance, nursing it till it becomes a spiritual monster, even if your anger about your abuse was originally just and holy. When this happens, you are in danger of entering into victimhood, in which being a victim of abuse becomes a life script, a full-time job, even a career. Anger then becomes a primary self-identity and a too-strong defense that blocks further growth and healing from your abuse or trauma.

I remember one counseling client who exemplified this very well. She came to me for counseling several years ago. She had been sexually abused as a child and had never dealt with its effects on her. She had been married to a basically good man who was kind to her, but who was emotionally distant and pre-occupied with his work and who died prematurely, leaving her a relatively young widow. Externally, she appeared to be very cordial, pleasant, and well put together, even spiritually. She had three adult children and a few grandchildren whom she saw with some frequency. She attended her church regularly and was engaged in numerous activities with her family, friends, and church. She came for counseling because she could never seem to enjoy any of this.

She was not clinically depressed, but after some exploration, I came to see that below her seemingly calm and pleasant exterior, she seethed with chronic, bitter anger about her life. She was angry about her childhood abuse and had projected much of that on her disappointing and now dead husband. She felt robbed by God of the closeness and intimacy that she craved. This was her grievance story. Because of this story, she held onto her anger in such a way that no one could really get close, not even her children and grandchildren. Externally, she observed her religion, but internally, she actually held a grudge and a grievance against God, keeping God at bay. There was no warmth, no closeness, no joy in anything that she did, including her religious activities. When I pointed all of this out to her and tried to help her see the relationships and joy that were available to her, she acknowledged her bitter anger, but could not see past it or relinquish it, despite the unhappiness it was causing her. She grimly held onto her grievance and anger, despite all that I attempted to do to encourage her to let go. Eventually, after several months of counseling, she just quit coming. I felt I never reached her or helped her see beyond her anger. I think about her periodically with great sadness, and I pray that she has found peace.

A psychologist named Stephen Karpman illustrates this in a different way, through his Karpman's Drama Triangle (See graphic on page 103) of Victim-Rescuer-Persecutor.

The Drama Triangle is fueled and driven by unresolved pain and anger. Each of these roles, if it becomes chronic, has an emotional pay-off. If you remain an unhealed victim, you can move to a rescuer position in relationships characterized by co-dependency and covert control and feel better about yourself through rescuing. Or it is just as possible for you to become an angry persecutor, a blamer in relationships, possibly even to the extent of becoming an abuser yourself in some fashion or form. The pay-off is the intoxication of power and the avoidance of your pain and of your old feeling of helplessness. Any survivor can switch to any of these three roles. Being stuck in any of them is unhealthy and damaging.

PERSECUTOR   RESCUER

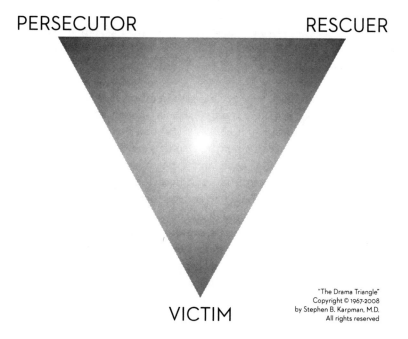

VICTIM

"The Drama Triangle"
Copyright © 1967-2008
by Stephen B. Karpman, M.D.
All rights reserved

Anger and its power are seductive. Your soul means for you to have your anger for a time to empower and heal you, and then, in your soul's time, to let it go. Anger can be addictive, however, and, if held onto past its expiration date, will actually eventually corrode and eviscerate your spiritual strengths and block your soul's path to your healing.

Mike describes the effects his chronic anger had on him through too much of his life:

As a small child I could never understand why I liked it better away from home. School and church were beacons of light and warmth. Domestic darkness and abuse on the home front prevailed however, and turned me into a frightened angry little man. I thought that going away to college 800 miles from home would change me. But I was putting old bitter wine into new wine skins, and soon discovered within a few short months of college that I brought all of the cynicism, bitterness and critical spirit with me.

No matter where I went, no matter what great friends I made, my fear-based anger seeped out at the seams. I criticized authority. I despised it. I scoffed at the wise and ridiculed the ignorant. I hated that part of me and was so filled with shame that I could never speak to a counselor or seek any real advice in spiritual direction. As I grew into adulthood, more and more people would shy away from my acidic personality. The loneliness and isolation ensued more and more. Acting out sexually, pornography, frustrated attempts at friendship and relationship, and idolizing those I wished to look like and be like became usual behaviors for me. Life grew more and more sterile. I was lost in a barren wilderness of anger.

Stuck anger can block your healing path in other ways as well. Anger can become a defense against other, more vulnerable emotions that you need to feel and move through in order to heal. Anger is always a secondary emotion arising from and covering over the primary emotions of fear, hurt, sadness, or some combination of all three. One or more of these emotions is always underneath your anger. As you will see on the Grief Pathway, it is necessary for your healing that you allow yourself to descend into and feel your hurt and your sadness. This allows your soul to move you through and out of your pain. Many people want to hold onto anger, once they access it, to avoid the pain and the vulnerability of grieving. It feels safer and stronger to remain angry and to not experience what is underneath. This too is seductive and dangerous, for the pathway of grief, sadness, and hurt is vital to your healing. Anger held tightly for too long can block you from entering this next healing path.

Paradoxically, the anger that is meant to help you break free from the power of your abuser, can, if held too long, keep you bound to him. I see this with some divorced individuals who remain virulently angry at their spouses years after the divorce. They expend enormous amounts of energy thinking about them, about how they have been wronged and hurt, and about what they would like to do to get back at them. They are still married to their despised spouse through their anger! Your own anger at your abuser, once it has done its soul work in freeing and empowering you, needs to be set free and released, so the tie with your abuser and his power over you is finally and irrevocably broken.

So what can you do if you are stuck in your anger? Listen to your soul. She will guide you. Be open to her quiet prompting when it is time to let go. She will let you know if your anger has become an obstacle. Ask your soul and ask God for the grace to surrender your anger against your abuser. This does not mean that you will have no anger at all. You will continue, as you should, to hate what your abuser did to you. But you will no longer hate your abuser or hold onto a grievance against life. Be open to begin the process of forgiveness, and take the first steps onto the Pathway of Forgiveness. Be honest with yourself about any unconscious pay-offs that you are getting from holding onto your anger, and ask for the grace to give them up as well. Your anger has served you well for a time and a season. It has helped to set you free. There comes a time, though, when your healing and your soul require you to let go and be free of your just and holy anger itself.

 Way Station

🔖 Repeat the Walking Meditation, again taking your anger about your abuse in your backpack. When you reach the mountaintop and the spiritual being appears, take out your anger and present it to him or her. Your spiritual guide will either take it from you if it is time to let go of your anger, or hand it back to you if you still need your anger. Let your soul and your spirit guide decide.

In your journal, pray about and reflect on the following questions:

Is your anger past its prime? Is it time to let go?

Has your anger stopped empowering you and started poisoning you?

Can you discern in yourself any signs of chronic bitterness, resentment, or even hate?

Have you become a person you wouldn't want to be friends with?

Do you nurse a grudge or obsess about your grievances?

🔖 What is your grievance story about your life? Write it out from the place of your deepest anger. List all of your grievances about your life. Notice what you feel when you read over your grievance story. Can you begin to change it and move beyond it? Rewrite it from a perspective of being ready to let go of your anger. Rewrite your grievance story and change it into a gratefulness story. What is right about your life? What can you be grateful for about you and your life? Notice how your gratefulness story feels to you. How is the feeling different than with your grievances? Can you begin to live more from your gratefulness than your grievance?

🔖 If it is time, and if you are ready, write a prayer of letting go of your anger and giving it to God. Thank God, thank your soul, thank holy anger itself for how it has served you in your healing. Then ask for the grace to choose to release the anger into God's hands. To the best of your ability, be open to receive that grace.

Congratulations again! You have completed the Pathway of Holy Anger. You are ready to step onto the Pathway of Grief. Pause for a while first, though, and look back on your sojourn with holy anger. Consider again what you have learned on this pathway and what has changed for you. Record these insights and changes in your journal.

PART FIVE

The Pathway of Grief

15

Grief as a Spiritual Retreat

You probably do not usually think of grief and sorrow as a blessing. These emotional states are painful, and we normally attempt to avoid and anesthetize their pain at all costs. This is one of the reasons that some victims try to hold onto the anger that covers and numbs the sadness and grief about their abuse. Yet there are indeed blessings hidden in the sorrow of grief. This is why allowing yourself to descend for a time into the sadness and suffering of grief and mourning is a necessary, although painful pathway to healing your spirit, broken and wounded by abuse.

One of the spiritual purposes of grief is to slow you down and pull you inward for a time so that you can own and feel what you have lost, sort out in your soul what these losses mean, renew and re-orient your shaken and broken spirit, and then eventually re-energize yourself to reinvest in your life in a new and more deeply soul-directed way. In a sense, grief is your soul's way of calling you to a spiritual retreat.

I saw grief drinking a cup of sorrow and called out, "It tastes sweet, does it not?" "You've caught me," grief answered, "and you've ruined my business, how can I sell sorrow when you know it's a blessing?"

—Rumi, Sufi mystical poet and saint, 1207-1273

I hope that you have had, or will take, the opportunity to experience a retreat. Spiritual retreats of several different kinds have been a vital feature of my life. In recent years, they have taken the form of going away for a weekend or a week to be by myself with God and my soul in a hermitage cabin at retreat centers either here in Missouri or in the mountains of Colorado. These are times when I can go inward without the usual distractions of my life. I can quiet my too-busy mind and schedule and listen to the whisperings of soul and Spirit. They are time-outs that enable me to sort out and try to make sense of the various changes and challenges of my life. At times, these retreats have been crucial in making major decisions in my life and ensuring that these decisions are soul and Spirit led. At other times, my retreats have involved slowing down to grieve what I have lost or what has changed along the way in my life journey.

This is the blessing your soul desires for you if you allow yourself to come away for a while. Your soul invites you to feel and listen to the grief that your abuse has engendered, a grief that may have been hidden inside of you for many years. Have you ever noticed that when you feel quite sad about something, or temporarily depressed (as opposed to clinical depression which is different and more serious), you have less energy, you feel lethargic, and your inclination is to curl up into a ball and escape from the world for a time? This is your body, your mind, and even your soul's attempt to slow you down, to pull you inward, and to send you on retreat to mourn, sort out, and heal your sadness or loss. We often ignore these invitations, submerge the sadness or grief, and plow on, avoiding the pain involved. The desire to avoid the pain is understandable. However, when you do this, you miss the soul-blessed opportunity to heal and to grow spiritually.

One of my teachers, Frederic Hudson, in *The Handbook of Coaching*, calls this slowing down and going inward, *cocooning*. He describes it as a necessary and natural chapter or phase in everyone's life. In his schema, when you are in touch with some significant loss, when there is an ending or major change in your life, when you are out of synch or feel disenchanted with your life, you enter into a phase Hudson terms *the doldrums*. If you pay attention to the sadness and diminished energy of the doldrums, you move into the phase of cocooning. This is a life chapter triggered and guided by your soul, a time for you to introspect, reflect, mourn, and search for new identity and meaning. For a victim of abuse or trauma, it is as if your soul invites you to withdraw within yourself for a period and wraps you up within a temporary cocoon of grief and sorrow about your pain and losses. This is so that you can eventually emerge from the grief cocoon as a new creation, with newly grown and beautifully colored wings, and fly.

> Blessed are the
> ones who mourn,
> for they will be
> comforted.
> —from *Matthew 5:4*

This cocooning or grief retreat can take on many forms. There are many trails for you to choose from on the Grief Pathway. You could decide to spend some time away from your usual schedule and environment and go someplace for a spiritual retreat of some kind, focusing on the losses you have incurred from your abuse or trauma. Or you may opt to do mini-retreats or Sabbath breaks in the midst of your normal life schedule, periodically carving out time and space to pray and journal about your losses. Grief has its own rhythms and seasons. You cannot exactly dictate or schedule your grieving. You can, however, make room for it in your life and give yourself permission to grieve so that it can arise as, and when, your soul knows is best for you.

It is vital too that you care for and nurture yourself well while you are in the cocoon of grief. Be particularly good to yourself. Pick and commit to at least three regular self-care activities. Pace yourself as well. The grief process does not have a time schedule. It does not have to be all at once or all or nothing. Your grief is something that you may want to focus on intensely for a time, or you may want to explore in short periods of grief work. This is a pathway that may take weeks, months, or even years, a pathway that you can step on and off as needed. Your soul will tell you what you need for yourself.

Since grief is a painful process, and since that pain can be overwhelming at times, it is important to take some precautions as you travel the Grief Pathway. This is a time when it is especially essential that you are sharing your healing journey with a spiritual guide or with a counselor, and with your *anam cara*, your soul friends. No one can grieve for you, and some of it needs to be done alone, yet grief is more healing, and you will move through it more quickly, if it is also shared. You do not need to be alone in your sadness and grieving. Share it with your therapist or spiritual guide. Share it with your soul friends. Start to bring your sadness before your soul and hear her response. In prayer and meditation, present your sadness and grief to God.

The first step onto the Grief Pathway is to begin to give yourself permission, time, and space to grieve your losses. Listen to your soul's call to move inward, to cocoon, to retreat, and to enter into the sadness and sorrow connected to your abuse. You need also to give yourself permission to start to let yourself feel your grief, to allow the emotions to surface.

One powerful way to tap into your grief is to read, meditate on, and pray the "sorrowful Psalms" from the Old Testament. This is an excellent way to begin to connect with the grief within you and also to help you to experience your grief as a spiritual process that can open you more deeply to your soul and to your God. Listen to and feel the deep emotion as the psalmist pours out his grief and sorrow in the following two Psalms:

> *How long, O Lord, will you utterly forget me. How long shall I harbor sorrow in my soul, grief in my heart, Day after day?*
> —*from Psalm 13:2-3*

> *As the deer longs for the running waters, so my soul longs for you, O Lord. Athirst is my soul for God, the living God. When shall I go and behold the face of God? My tears are my food day and night, as they say to me day after day, "Where is your God?"*
> *Why are you so downcast, O my soul? Why do you sigh within me?*
> *Hope in God! For I shall again be thanking him in the presence of my savior and my God*
> —*from Psalm 42:2-4, 6,*

As you peer into the grief box inside you, you will likely experience considerable resistance from parts of your self. It may appear to you that your grief is Pandora's box, not a source of blessing and healing. You will not want to feel its pain. This is an understandable response. None of us wants to be in pain. The Grief Pathway is a time, though, to trust your soul that your sorrow will lead to consolation and that your grief will lead to joy.

> *Those that sow in tears shall reap rejoicing.*
> *Although they go forth weeping, carrying the seed to be sown,*
> *They shall come back rejoicing, carrying their sheaves.*
> —*from Psalm 126:5-6*

 ## *Way Station*

In your journal, reflect on the following questions:
What do you feel when you contemplate allowing yourself to grieve?
Do you sense any resistance or fear within you?
Do you detect any part of you that believes that you are being too self-focused, self-pitying, or selfish if you spend this time with your losses?
What will you need for yourself, from yourself and your soul, to overcome any resistance or fear of your sadness and grief?

In your journal, outline a specific self-care plan for yourself for when you are in your grief. Make it concrete, doable, accountable, and measurable. In other words, how will you know that you are taking good care of yourself, and who will know this besides yourself?

Spend some time considering, and at least loosely planning, how you will allow yourself time and space for your grief retreat and cocooning. What will your cocoon look like? Do you want to go away to a retreat center? Do you want to set aside some time in your regular schedule to go into the sacred space you created for yourself at the beginning of this book, so that you can enter into and journal your grief?

Read and reflect on any of the sorrowful Psalms: 5, 6, 13, 14, 22, 31, 39, 63, 69, 77, 88, 102, 116, 126, and 139. In your journal, write about how they touch you. What emotions do they invoke in you? How does it feel to bring your sadness before your soul and before God, as the psalmist does?

Write your own broken-heart prayer expressing your sorrow, sadness, and grief about your abuse. Address it to your soul or to God. Pray it daily for a week or as long as you need to in order to fully access and feel your grief.

Journal

As a survivor of abuse and trauma, you have suffered many losses as a result of your experiences. Grief about those losses is painful and hardly seems a blessing. In this next selection from her journal, Vicki shares her own pain and grief and how they became a life-giving spiritual gift for her.

From Vicki's Journal—

As long as I was suffering in silence, holding the expansiveness of the pain inside, I was forced to remain stuck in the intensity of grief. As soon as I could speak the pain that was locked in my heart to my therapist, I could begin the healing process that I needed. When I began to break the silence, to share the pain of the story with a sacred circle of friends and family, I could then begin to grieve.

Once while attending a conference in Albuquerque, New Mexico, a Liturgy of Lamentations was being held. The liturgy began with a Jewish woman wailing, and it continued piercing through the silence of a room filled with 1,200 people. The entire group lamented with great anguish all the injustice and suffering in the world around us: the war in Iraq, the hungry, the poor, women who are used as weapons of war, human trafficking—and I was lamenting my own pain and all that I had lost. The liturgy continued with a physical ritual of grinding corn. The grinding of the corn symbolized less of me and more of God. I prayed that mantra, less of me and more of God, repeatedly.

It is a different kind of grief than the loss of someone you love deeply. In my case, the loss of my identity was paramount. When I realized what I had lost, I mourned the loss profoundly. It was a deep pain I had never before felt. And yet, in the midst of that process, I knew the only way to heal it was to emote my way through it, to feel it, to claim it, and to set it free. The "setting free" part seemed interminably long. Once I claimed the grief as my own, I think I had to wallow in its bitterness for a while. I remember immersing myself in my work during that period. Keeping inordinately busy and absorbed with a busy life masked my grief for a time, even after I claimed it. There was also a season of arrogant self-righteousness that later haunted me. In the midst of my grief and the stages of anger that I experienced, I felt the fullness of having been victimized. Self-righteousness became the outward sign of still deeper issues that needed to be addressed and grieved. The self-righteousness would be expressed as I spoke about my abuser to trusted friends and denounced and demonized him in ways that I would never consider doing today. The patience and love of a few trusted friends made a huge difference as I grieved.

Once I began to understand what I had lost in fourteen years of abuse, I began again to grieve and mourn my loss of self. The awareness of the amount of my life that I had given to my abuser was overwhelming at times. The painful process of restoring my "self" felt like a mammoth effort, a monumental task, a weight that was perilously drowning me. I grieved the loss of the freedom to follow my true path, God's call for me. I did not feel free to make my own decisions. I acutely grieved the loss of having my own children, of growing along the same path as my peers, pursuing higher education, and marrying in my 20's, of starting my own family, or the joy of giving grandchildren to my parents. As time moved on, and I've grown into those years when I would normally have begun to have grandchildren, the sting of that loss again rears its ugly head. I see my peers and my brother enjoying their grandchildren with a love that I will never know. Oh, I love my nieces and nephews more than I can say. But, I will never experience the true joy of being a grandparent. This is a huge issue for me even today.

After the abuse stopped and the grief was at its ripest stage, I spent time working in Los Angeles with the homeless. I stayed with an order of Brothers founded by Mother Teresa. They have a large mission to the homeless in Los Angeles. By this time, I really felt broken and useless. However, it was the immersion with the homeless, the destitute on those rough streets, that brought me into the path of descent where real transformation happens. Some call it liminal space, where one is in the midst of chaos just waiting to emerge on the other side of an experience. A homeless woman named Marguerite became a healing angel for me as I ministered to her through her illness on a filthy mattress near an abandoned hotel. Her brokenness mirrored my own emotional state. She taught me, without any words, that while I may have been justified in my pain, indeed, the time had come for me to climb out of grief and begin living for others. The scene of sitting next to her one evening at 10 p.m. and praying with her in such an unlikely environment, under a scraggly old tree in the middle of downtown Los Angeles, will long be a reminder of that healing.

Richard Rohr's teaching on the path of descent and Joan Chittister's writing on struggle helped me to find a way to transform the grief into something meaningful and useful. They empowered me to see the wisdom that was rising out of the suffering. Rohr's classic spiritual teaching explains the power of struggle as a way toward transformation. The path of descent calls us to cry out, "more of God, less of me"—the grinding of corn into corn meal. In weakness, we can truly find the path to transformation. I believe it is the only way to real transformation. I have learned much about life and love and death and sorrow. They are my real spiritual teachers.

In The Bond between Women *by China Galland, she speaks eloquently about the goodness and wisdom that arise within us to overcome any number of obstacles:*

There is a goodness, a Wisdom that arises, sometimes gracefully, sometimes gently, sometimes awkwardly, sometimes fiercely, but it will arise to save us if we let it, and it arises from within us, like the force that drives green shoots to break the winter ground, it will arise and drive us into a great blossoming like a pear tree, into flowering, into fragrance, fruit, and song, into the wild wind dancing, sun shimmering, into the aliveness of it all, into that part of ourselves that can never be defiled, defeated, or destroyed, but that comes back to life, time and time again, that lives—always—that does not die.

I knew I had to create a greater spaciousness to hold my grief. At times, the grief was weakening of mind, body and spirit. Those late night drives home when I considered running into bridge abutments were reflective of how grief weakened me during the darkest times. It was my faith, though, my deep trust in God's amazing love for me, that buoyed me during those darkest moments. My therapist played a significant role in convincing me anew that God loved me and saw me as a precious daughter. She affirmed me as a person of value when I was mocked as psychologically unfit. And because of the level of trust between us, because of how she modeled the unconditional love of God, I could tangibly integrate that solid understanding into my own soul. I could believe that, indeed, I was psychologically sound.

All of us have icons of courage that we have identified in our lives. Perhaps we carry images of those heroic people in our heart that help inform our own lives. It is easy to look outside ourselves and readily acknowledge the heroic actions of others. It is much more difficult to see the small courageous steps that we take. Mother Teresa of Calcutta was a courageous figure for me. The example of her life, her commitment to saving just that one that was dying on the streets of Calcutta, was archetypal for me. Mother often talked about the countries in the West being much more difficult to serve. In India, she could offer rice and dahl to the poor. In Europe and the United States, the problems of the poor were more challenging. They did not want for lack of food, but for lack of love. The alcoholics and drug addicts she encountered in every major city in our country convinced her that their poverty was a poverty of love. Mother Teresa never looked at the masses that needed her help, she looked at just that one in front of her. Thankfully, I was not an alcoholic or an addict. However, I came to understand that I too was just that one that needed to be saved.

A principal moment in my grieving process came in a visit with Mother Teresa that had been encouraged by my therapist. When Mother Teresa came into the room where we were to meet in Washington, D.C., I remember feeling guilty that I had added this meeting to her busy schedule. Mother put me at ease quickly though. She entered the room in her quiet and humble way, came to me with her hands folded in the traditional Bengali namaste greeting, and invited me to sit with her. I shared with her the process of healing I was undertaking after an abusive relationship with a priest. Although her words were difficult to hear in that moment, her words were both calming and prophetic. The first thing that she said was, "We must pray for our priests. We must trust and have confidence that Jesus walks with us through everything, that our suffering was his suffering first." She also said something that I had heard her say so often before, "When we are suffering so much, it is Jesus that is kissing us. We may want to tell Jesus to stop kissing us, but he knows it is the way to holiness."

Asking me to pray for priests was, at that time, a most difficult request to honor. As time passed and healing continued, I came to understand the wisdom of all her words. The Gospel of Jesus calls us to pray for everyone, even those who have abused others. Indeed, it was the most broken and despised that Jesus surrounded himself with in his

short time on earth. Later in my journey, I would come to understand Mother Teresa's
plea for me to pray for priests.

A few years later, on a mission trip to Mexico, the group I was traveling with
visited a small rancho along a busy trans-continental highway. It is called Kilometer
29 and identifies the group of women settled along the highway. In order to support
themselves and feed their children, they began prostituting themselves to the truck-
ers who occasionally visited. The diminutive rancho populated only with women and
children reflected their desperate poverty. We developed a relationship with the women
over time and, on this particular visit, felt called to find a way to reach the deep pain
we knew they harbored because of their life of prostitution. After reflection, we created
a prayer service that would include the sharing of our own personal stories of abuse
and pain. Within our group of twenty, three women, including myself, were willing
to share their stories in a way that would help the Mexican women get in touch with
their own stories and pain.

Our stories would need to be presented in a way that did not confront or judge.
They would reflect the fear of telling the story, the pain of living the story, and the
experience of healing. I chose to share in this way:

> During a very difficult time in my life, I lived under the control of
> a man who abused me emotionally and sexually. His control in my
> life kept me from marrying and having a family of my own.
> This was something that I longed for deeply.
> When I was baptized, God lit a holy lamp in my heart.
> The relationship with this man caused that light to grow dim.
> After a time, I was able to remove myself from this abusive
> relationship, and I began to heal from the pain. Today, after much
> healing, the holy lamp in my heart is burning brightly again.

After sharing my story in this way, the woman who sat at my left threw her arms
around me and openly wept. We both wept. We held each other in an embrace only two
women could understand. With that embrace, we held each other's pain in an intimate
and loving way. No words were spoken, and yet we understood each other completely.

Today, I understand grief as a necessary part of living. All of life is a letting go, a
spirituality of subtraction, as Richard Rohr says. After seeing how God's grace works
faithfully in my daily life, I now accept all that life offers, trusting always. Every
experience leads us to the next experience. Every resounding "YES" to God lays the
groundwork for the next experience. I can live in gratitude now, for every experience,
even the ones that hurt the most. There are lessons upon lessons to be assimilated in all
of it.

16

Naming and Mourning the Losses of Your Spirit

As a survivor of abuse, you have a lot to grieve for. There are many losses that abuse has inflicted on you, both psychological and spiritual. There are many things in your life that your abuser has, in effect, stolen from you. This chapter is about naming and mourning these losses. The grief about your abuse that you will feel in this cocooning time is similar to and yet in some ways different from the grief that you experience when a loved one dies. Many of the emotions are the same: a deep sadness and feeling of loss, a feeling of emptiness in your life, a sensation of disorientation and confusion about your self and your life, and periods of lowered mood and energy.

When a loved one dies, the loss is often clear, and the pain is usually focused. With grief about abuse, the pain can be just as intense, but it is often vague and diffused, and the losses involved less obvious. Part of the task and blessing of the Grief Pathway is being able to name, and so being able to properly mourn, your losses, to fully grieve what abuse and your abuser have taken from you. This in time will help you to move beyond and be free of your pain. This is not an intellectual or primarily cognitive process. For grief to be healing, it has to be felt. In fact, allowing yourself to mourn and feel your grief can be a key breakthrough in restoring your ability to feel your emotions. For some victims, perhaps for you,

> But the soul has no culture. The soul has no nations. The soul has no colour or accent or way of life. The soul is forever. The soul is one. And when the heart has its moment of truth and sorrow, the soul can't be stilled...And some things are just so sad that only your soul can do the crying for you.
>
> —from Gregory David Roberts's *Shantaram*

one of the losses that abuse has taken is the very vital human capacity to fully feel and experience emotions. Grief itself helps to restore this loss.

A key spiritual purpose of grief is to free you from the hold and oppression of the past. If you still live controlled and haunted by the events of the past, especially past abuse, then you have less energy for your life in the present. In fact, you are not living in the now of your life. You are driving forward through your life by looking in the rear view mirror—a dangerous way to drive. You are also trudging through life with very heavy baggage that no longer fits for you and is no longer useful. It simply weighs you down and keeps pulling you back to the past. Grief in the Spirit puts the past in the past and prepares you to move into a new future.

Paradoxically, before you can let it go and be in your now, grief requires you to first revisit and mourn the past. I am frequently asked by my clients in counseling, "Why do I need to explore my past. I want to forget the pain that I went through then. Why dredge it all up again?" If the past is truly past, and it no longer affects you, then, indeed, there is no reason to go back there. However, for many survivors of abuse, the past is still very much present and alive in them, impacting them in a variety of significant ways. Until it is faced, felt, and understood, the past continues to haunt and overshadow your present life and functioning.

Grief is part of the process of revisiting the past, so that you are freed from it and no longer live partially or wholly in your past. It may seem silly to cry over events that happened long ago, but buried grief is toxic for you, and if not honored and allowed expression, it limits your spirit's capacity for joy, hope, and love. As Ellen Bass and Laura Davis write in their classic book on healing from abuse, *The Courage to Heal*:

> As children being abused, and later as adults struggling to survive, most survivors haven't felt their losses. Grieving is a way to honor your pain, let go, and move into the present.

Mike beautifully describes and summarizes the spiritual process of the Grief Pathway and its role in shedding the past as he shares his own journey through grief:

> When I went away for inpatient treatment, my grief ran deep. I mourned and grieved for what my multiple childhood abuses had taken from me. I was learning to gently lay aside old habits and patterns of survival that just did not fit anymore. Like shedding old skin, the painful process of changing from blaming to listening, from defensiveness to acceptance, from dying to being born again stretched me more and more, but I had to do it. It was like setting aside a pair of old, tight fitting boots that never fit. For years I lived with the discomfort of not fitting

*into my real self, but was too unskilled and afraid to change. I finally
began to learn that it would demand trust to set aside what didn't fit
anymore, and try on the new boots that actually worked. I began to see
myself as never before.*

There are a number of ways to explain how the past impacts us in the present, including a growing understanding of how trauma and abuse are stored in
the various structures of the brain and even shape and re-wire the brain, altering
some of its functioning. The spiritual writer Eckhart Tolle, in his book, *Practic-
ing the Power of Now*, provides a description of the power of the past in his
concept of the "pain-body":

> *Pain-body is an energy field, almost like an entity, that has become
> temporarily lodged in your inner space. It is life energy that has become
> trapped, energy that is no longer flowing. Of course, the pain body is
> there because of certain things that happened in the past. It is the living
> past in you, and if you identify with it, you identify with the past.*

Unhealed abuse and trauma burden the survivor with a heavy load of pain-
body that is experienced physically, emotionally, and also spiritually. Your heart
is heavy with sorrow, your life energy diminished, and a darkened veil hangs
between you and your soul. The power of the pain-body is in unconsciously
identifying with the pain. It is rooted in believing that what was done to you in
the abuse, and the wounds that you carry from it, are truly you, and define and
limit you. It is the belief that what your abuser did to you created who you are,
even in your essence, even spiritually.

Grief in the Spirit is a process for dissolving the pain-body and ending your
identification with the pain of your trauma or abuse. It combines both psychological and spiritual processes. It is the soul-led journey of grief. It is an inner
movement guided by your soul with four phases:

The first involves bringing your buried pain-body grief into consciousness by
allowing yourself to feel the sorrow and sadness of your losses and being present
to your pain without analysis or judgment.

In the second phase, you invite an inner witness, what Tolle calls your
"watcher," to witness and name your pain-body and see that it is the residue of
your abuse and not who you are. The witness can be an inner observer part of
you, your capacity for self-consciousness, or even your soul itself. Your soul will
always be present with you as you grieve, grieving with and for you, sometimes
crying on your behalf when the pain is deep for you to cry for yourself.

The mourning and witnessing, in time, dissolve, and, in the third phase, they
heal the pain-body grief, especially as you continue to break your identification
with the pain and losses from your trauma or abuse.

In the final phase, the grief and mourning gradually give way to a new energy to refocus, renew, and reinvest yourself in your life in ways before unimaginable. As Mike put it, you are shedding an old skin that no longer fits and growing into a new skin that truly befits who you are in your True Self.

This is a meditation process, not a cognitive or thought process. It is described in more detail in the following Way Station. It involves allowing yourself, in a meditative state, to feel your pain-body, feel the losses from your abuse—in other words, to mourn—and then bring it into consciousness by being fully present to it. As you feel your grief and pain, your inner witness, accompanied by your soul, is able to watch and name your pain and your loss without judgment and see that it is your abuse and not you. This breaks your identification with your pain. Your soul knows who you are and who you are not. You are not what you have lost, what has been taken from you, or what was done to you. What you name, your soul can tame. What you mourn, you can in time let go of so that you can be renewed and be free.

 ## *Way Station*

To help you begin to be in touch with the losses and grief inflicted on you by your abuse, reflect on and journal about the following questions. They will bring your buried grief to the surface. Your losses involve your whole self and are emotional-psychological, relational, and spiritual. To be more aware of the spiritual losses, you might find it helpful to review the list of soul wounds in Chapter Three and *The Spiritual Laundry List—The The Grease, Grit, & Grime* in Chapter Four.

What would my life, including my spiritual life, have been like if I had not experienced abuse?

What normal growing up experiences did I get robbed of?

What life opportunities were stolen from me?

How would my life be different without the abuse?

How would I be different?

What parts of me have had to be buried or underdeveloped because of the abuse?

What relationships have I lost?

What life dreams have I given up or put on hold?

What have I lost spiritually?

How much trust, faith, or hope has been drained from me by my abuse?

How would my relationship with my soul and with the God of my understanding be different now?

To what degree have I, at least for now, lost my ability to feel valued and loved by God or by my soul?

How has the abuse affected my relationship with prayer, worship, or church communities?

What has abuse taken from my life-vision and sense of personal life-purpose?

🔖 Do a free writing or stream-of-consciousness exercise about your losses. Take a few moments to center or pray using the method, like focusing on your breath or repeating a prayer phrase, that works best for you. Then take your journal and a pen, set a timer for twenty minutes, and begin to write down all of the losses from your abuse that come to your mind. Don't edit or analyze what you are writing. Don't worry about punctuation, spelling, grammar, or doing it right. Just allow your losses to stream out of you onto the paper until the timer goes off.

Next, go back over your writing, your list of losses, and pick out the ten most impactful or painful losses. Let your intuition guide you. There is no need to prioritize them from one to ten.

Then, gradually over time, one by one, bring each of these losses to meditation or prayer:

First, center yourself by focusing on your breath or some short prayer, inviting yourself to a place of safety and peace deep inside you. This can be done with eyes closed or open, whichever feels most comfortable to you.

Then bring to mind one of the losses. Allow yourself to feel the grief and pain of that loss. Be aware of what abuse has cost you in this area. Notice what images, emotions, memories, or symbols emerge into your awareness. Focus periodically back on your breathing or your prayer. Re-center on your breath or your emotion if you start to flee to your head, especially if you start to judge yourself. If the emotion becomes overwhelming, give yourself permission to end for now and return to the meditation at another time. Self-care is always first.

At some point in your meditation, invite your inner witness to be present to your grief about the loss. If the inner witness is someone other than your soul, make sure that you envision your soul's presence as well. If it fits for you, invite God to be present too. (It's alright if it gets a bit crowded inside you—better than being alone with your grief!). Be aware of what your witness sees about your loss; be aware of your loss from the viewpoint of your soul. Feel compassion for your loss. Hear your soul, or your God, whispering to you:

> *I am so sorry you endured this pain and suffered this loss.*
> *I cry with you. I mourn for what was taken from you.*
> *This is not the end of your story. I will help to restore you and what*
> *you have lost in a new way. This pain, these losses, are not all of who you*
> *are. They are not you at all. Come, I will show you who you truly are.*

Bring your meditation to a close by again focusing on your breath or prayer, relaxing the muscles of your body. On each exhale, release every molecule of the grief pain that you experienced in the meditation.

Record in your journal what you experienced and learned.

Make sure that you create a time to share your grief experiences on this pathway with your therapist, pastor, or other spiritual mentor and with your soul-friends. Let them grieve and mourn with you.

Journal

Sue names her own losses in this next section. Perhaps her losses are similar to yours. Perhaps your losses to abuse and trauma are different. The grief is shared and the pathway through grief to healing and triumph over your losses is universal.

From Sue's Journal—

Perhaps the greatest hurt that I experienced from Monsignor's actions was the effect of the abuse on my mother. Her behavior sometimes became erratic and unpredictable. She had outbursts of unexplained hysteria and extreme anxiety. This deeply wounded my parents' marriage. From four on, I became my mother's guardian and caretaker. It was my job to take care of her for my father when she was distraught, and my father did not know what to do with her. So all that was wounded in my mother by our common trauma affected me deeply.

Despite her unhealed trauma, my Mother at other times was a loving, attentive, caring mom who worked hard to care for our needs. She was a miracle worker in the kitchen parlaying our limited food budget into home-baked breads, cakes, pies, jams, and jellies that fed our tummies and our hearts with nourishing caloric love. Her soul shined especially brightly through her pain when she played the piano for us, bringing the joy of music to our house. My greatest sadness about what happened is that my mother never received any help for her trauma from this incident with Monsignor.

During and after my primal scream period, much grief about my life surfaced: loss of an emotionally healthy mom; loss of my childhood in many ways, since I became my mom's caretaker; the sadness and humiliation of mom's erratic, irrational, hysterical outbursts and behavior; the opportunities that I missed as a child to be open, and free, and visible. I began, too, to grieve things missing in my adult life. There were far too many possibilities never realized, healthy paths never chosen, or those that I had allowed to be blocked.

In my forties, I pursued several years of professional training and personal and spiritual growth work with my mentor and pioneer family therapist, Virginia Satir. In a sense, it was a year-long spiritual retreat to allow God to help me discover the hidden person that I always was. There were periods during this time of great joy, of exciting discovery, and personal breakthroughs. It was also, off and on, a time of great grief, especially about what might have been. I grieved and ended my first marriage. I grieved, for the first time, the deaths at childbirth of two of my children. I grieved the constrained and fearful life that in some ways I had led since I was four. However, I emerged from this long passage of my life a new person—really, though, the person that I had always invisibly been—with a new life. This is the life that I live now and have been living gratefully, joyfully for many years.

17

Reclaiming and Restoring Your Spirit

I recently completed a very difficult course of grief therapy with a woman in her late 60's. Let's call her Colleen. Colleen's grief had been profound and complicated and took a considerable amount of time to move through and finish. The loss of her husband was painful enough. After his death, she discovered some secrets about him that he had kept from her. These disclosures compounded her grief, profoundly shocking her and shattering her image of her husband, their marriage, and even of herself. She came to realize that in some ways her marriage had been abusive. She was shaken to her foundations by her grief and the revelations that attended her loss.

For months, Colleen struggled to regain her footing, and make sense of what she had lost both through her husband's death and because of this new information about him. Her mind went around and around seeking to make sense of what had happened. Her emotions swirled from anger at her husband, to deep sadness, to profound confusion. She hated what he had done, and still, at the same time, she missed him dearly each moment of each day. She became mired in grief, depression, and psychological and spiritual disorientation. I became concerned that I might not be able to help her to lift herself out of this.

The turning point came when I was inspired to help Colleen rediscover and restore two things that she had lost in the busyness and dysfunction of her life with her husband and their children. The inspiration for the first came when I suggested to Colleen that she might find more spiritual solace and a renewed faith if she returned to the faith community that she had left behind to please her husband. When she left her husband's church to reconnect with her own, she rediscovered a spiritual connection with her soul and with God that she had somewhat lost.

The second thing that Colleen tapped into was a sense of self and purpose that she had once possessed through a very extensive and successful professional career. She had subordinated her career to the jealous dominance of her very driven husband and to the understandable needs of their children. As she rediscovered her spiritual home and began to be spiritually nourished there, and as she reclaimed the threads of her life purpose and sense of self through revisiting the personal strengths of her career, she began to emerge from the grief. She decided to volunteer for an institution that she had once worked in. She had more energy and motivation to be involved with and enjoy her children and grandchildren. She still missed her husband and still loved him despite what he had hidden from her, but she was moving on and shaping a new life for herself from the ashes of her very painful grief.

Grief, especially the delayed grief that victims of abuse often experience, can deeply shake a person's sense of self and meaning. Major losses in your life may shake you to your foundations. This is certainly true of the losses imposed by abuse. You may find yourself asking: Who am I now? What is real? What is left? What is meaningful? What is my life purpose now? Where do I go with my life now? These are deeply spiritual questions. In raising these questions, grief challenges you to eventually re-orient and re-energize yourself and your life in relationship to your losses. This is another aspect of the deep soul work of grief.

These existential questions incubate in the cocoon of your grief. Your soul helps you to turn them over and over as they are polished like rough-cut gemstones placed in a rock tumbler until they are smooth and shine in the light. Gradually, answers appear out of the gloomy fog of your grief. Some of them will be new answers, some of them will be old answers now seen in a new light, with an added dimension or a new twist. As these answers emerge, and as you start to free yourself from the past through the expression and release of your grief, you will begin to find a new energy percolating up from deep within you. This is the energy of your soul stirring you to set out in new directions, to re-invest yourself back into your life with new vigor and new vision.

When you are in the midst of your grief, it is hard to believe that you will ever come out of the pit that you feel you have fallen into. It is equally difficult to trust that any light or goodness will emerge from the darkness of your grief. The dawn, though, will surely follow the night. New life and personal resurrection will in time come forth from the cocooning period of your grief. Especially when the grief process is painful, dark, and slow, it is tempting to lose hope and to abandon trust that light is coming or that God and your soul are at work in your grief. The prophet Habakkuk addresses this feeling and provides a basis for hope when he writes of his own spiritual struggle:

> *How long, O Lord? I cry for help, but you do not listen!*
> *I cry out to you, "Violence!", but you do not intervene.*
> *Why do you let me see ruin? Why must I look at misery?*
> *Then the Lord answered me and said:*
> *Write down the vision clearly upon the tablets,*
> *So that one can read it readily.*
> *For the vision still has its time, presses on to fulfillment,*
> *And will not disappoint; if it delays, wait for it,*
> *It will surely come, it will not be late.*
> *—from Habakkuk 1:2-3, 2:2-3*

In this especially spiritual part of your grief in the Spirit, guided by your soul, you can create a new vision for yourself and your life. You can embark upon the process of restoring the lost pieces of your broken spirit that you have been mourning. You can rebuild your spirituality on new foundations and without the wounds and distortions from your abuse. You will discover spiritual gifts arising from your grief, some of them coming from the abuse wounds and losses themselves. (This will become clearer and more concrete to you when you travel the Transformation Pathway in Part Seven.)

The movement through grief to a new spiritual vision of your self also aids in the process of moving from the mode of victim, to survivor, and eventually to thriver. Helen illustrates this well, describing her experience of spiritual gifts arising from grief, when she writes to her abuser about her own grief process:

> *The last twelve years of my life have been a mourning process. I have mourned the loss of my innocence, my childhood, and the world that I created around me that I felt would keep me from being manipulated again. The mourning is over. Today I am a thirty-seven year old woman who can look back on that experience (of childhood rape), and know that it wasn't my fault. I know that I didn't do anything to deserve your abuse. Evil triumphed in your heart that day, but not in mine. While I can list all of the things that you robbed me of, I can now also list the gifts that came from that experience. For instance, from that experience, I grew to be a more compassionate person, rather than angry, closed up, and resentful.*

Although the Grief Pathway is an important part of the spiritual healing process, and although it is necessary often to give yourself a significant amount of time on this pathway, there is also a danger of getting stuck here in your grief. On the Anger Pathway, we looked at the damage that can be caused by getting stuck in your anger. The potential damage of being stuck in your grief over your abuse is that you can become mired in chronic sadness, sorrow, and even spiritual despair. This drains your energy, saps your spirit, and has the potential to place you into life-long victimhood, a psychological and spiritual space of permanent negativity, shame, bitterness, assumed helplessness, and vulnerability to further abuse.

The pull and gravity of the past is quite powerful. The pull of what is familiar to you, even if it is misery, is very difficult to resist. It can feel overwhelming and can even invoke great fear. It is intimidating to trust your soul as she whispers to you to let go of old beliefs, patterns, and walls and defenses that you erected to protect yourself but that are now in your way. Grief requires you to revisit and live in the past for a time, but its emotional and spiritual purpose is really to empower you to put the past behind you and to begin to fashion and move into a new future relatively free of the past. It will take the spiritual courage that you developed on the first pathway to accomplish this.

Your soul has a further way to help you—ritual. Rituals are spiritually powerful ways to express and release your grief through sign, symbol, words, your senses, movement, and symbolic actions. Rituals can be public and rooted in centuries of cultural and religious tradition. Or they can be personal, private rituals that you create to express your grief and share with a few close soul friends or only with God and your soul. The use of symbol and action in ritual reaches deeper into your spirit than mere words or concepts can do and helps to both express and release grief from a central core of your being. Ritual creates a sacred space for you to honor and healthfully express the pain and losses from your abuse. It can help make your suffering redemptive, rather than paralyzing. Personal grief rituals can be especially impactful when you are ready to release and let go of the past and its losses. Ritual, like burning incense, lifts grief up into a higher spiritual plane, where it is taken up and away.

My family has a knack for funerals. Perhaps it is our Irish Catholic background that helps us to put together rituals that are both communal and personal, poetic and sacramental, sacred and funny, that help us to both joyfully celebrate the life of our family members and to mourn and grieve our losses in a way that is uplifting. At one of our last funerals, at the death of my beloved older brother, Rocky, one of my sister's friends was so moved that she was heard to say, "I want to go first!" before any of us, so that we could conduct her funeral in a similar spirit. Ritual, done well, drawing on both the personal and the sacred, can be that powerful.

Several years ago, Sue and I traveled to the beautiful Colorado mountain community of Crested Butte in the autumn to experience the spectacular beauty of the aspen trees turning gold on the mountainsides. The town was having its fall festival, which included an annual ritual, apparently derived from an old Slavic tradition, called "Burning the Grump." This involved building a large bonfire in the center of the town with Mount Crested Butte as the backdrop. When the bonfire was lit and burning fiercely, the scarecrow-like figure of the Grump was thrown on the fire to be burned up. The Grump represented all of our losses, sorrows, resentments, grudges, conflicts, and regrets of the past year. Its burning symbolized the choice to let go of all of these so that we could start fresh for a new year.

As the Grump smoldered, everyone in the circle around the fire was invited to throw onto the pyre any object that would more personally symbolize the "grumps" of each individual. There was, at first, relative silence as we all threw our symbols into the fire, the main sound the crackling of the flames, and then a great cheer went up as we watched our grumps being consumed and destroyed by the great fire. At some point in your healing process, it will be time for you to "burn the grump," to express, finish, and let go of your grief. Only you, your soul, and the Spirit know when that time will be. When it is time, a personal ritual created by you, and perhaps shared with your soul friends, will help you to do this.

Our abuse clients have designed and performed all sorts of rituals to aid their healing journeys. Some have performed a similar burning ritual: they put symbols or words on paper, representing the losses from their trauma or abuse, in a fire blessed with prayer and the presence of friends. Other clients have used the ritual of burial to symbolize something that has died in their life because of the trauma or abuse, such as the innocence of childhood prematurely snatched away by abuse. Still others have released balloons to mark the end and release of their grief. Several designed rituals in which they bathed in the ocean, lake, stream, bathtub, or pool to ritualize a baptismal-like cleansing from the effects of abuse. Some survivors have gone to an Easter service, or planted a tree or a spring flower, to express the new life that their grief was now yielding to. There are a myriad of life-giving, grief-expressing rituals that you can create and that fit you and your particular need to signify your grief journey. There is an exercise in the next Way Station that can help you put such a ritual together for yourself. Again, your soul will guide you. Listen to her voice, and together you will be inspired to create a ritual of your own.

 Way Station

🖎 Repeat the Walking Meditation as you did on previous pathways. For this trip up the mountain, put your list of losses that you prepared in the last section in your backpack and present them to the spiritual being you encounter on top of the mountain. Be aware of the response you receive, and of what you feel about your losses in the presence of the being. Listen to what you are invited to do with your bag of grief. Notice if anything changes for you in regard to your losses. Record your experience in your journal.

🖎 Create a ritual for yourself. While rituals are particularly helpful on the Grief Pathway, they can be created for your journey along any of the Five Pathways. You can choose an established ritual from your own faith tradition and community, create your own, or design a ritual that draws from both. To create a personal ritual, decide on a specific time and place that has sacred or special meaning to you. Choose symbols, words, and activities that have significance to you. You can do your ritual alone, with your soul friends, or in some public venue like a church, temple or synagogue—whatever best helps you to express and journey through your grief.

The following reflection questions can help you develop and plan your ritual:

What is the loss, event, or experience that you want to mark by entering into the ritual?

What would best express this for you?

What will be the theme of the ritual?

What tone and mood do you want to set?

Are there any particular symbols or special objects that you want to include in your ritual, such as photos, clothing, mementos, objects from nature, religious objects or symbols?

Do you want your ritual to include storytelling, poetry, readings from your journal, or excerpts from spiritual and sacred writings?

Is there any sort of movement or dance that you want to be part of the ritual?

Who do you want to participate in the ritual?

Who do you want to witness the ritual?

Where do you want the ritual to take place? What kind of place would be most sacred to you? Indoors or outdoors?

When you have prayerfully reflected on these questions, set aside time to put your ritual together. It can be as simple or multi-faceted as you want it to be. Then set a time and place and perform your ritual. Spend time later, and meditate on your experience of your ritual, eventually recording how it moved you and what it changed for you in your journal. The ritual can be repeated as often, and in is many different forms, as you want. Its meaning and format may evolve over time as your grief evolves and changes according to your journey and your need.

🖋 You have completed another of the pathways. Affirm yourself for your courage, for your determination, and for all of the healing spiritual work that you are doing for yourself. Your soul is proud of you and invites you to be proud of you as well. Take some time for prayer or meditation, and listen for God and your soul congratulating you and rejoicing with you.

🖋 Spend some time reflecting on your journey on the Pathway of Grief and record your thoughts in your journal. Then be ready to move onto the next stage of your pilgrimage, the Pathway of Forgiveness.

What has shifted or changed within you as a result of your time in the cocoon of grief in the Spirit?

What baggage from the past do you sense that you now no longer carry?

What new energy do you now experience within you?

What is the new vision that is beginning to form for you and your life?

What can you see that God and your soul have done for you on the Grief Pathway?

PART SIX

The Pathway of Forgiveness

18

Forgiveness is First for the Forgiver: The Power of Forgiveness to Heal Your Spirit

A s a victim of abuse, you may have been avoiding this pathway, the Path of Forgiveness. In many ways, it is the most difficult of the Five Pathways. You may even be angry that we are suggesting it as a vital part of your spiritual healing. Your feelings are understandable. In response to the great harm done by abuse—especially childhood abuse—forgiveness is very difficult and can even feel wrong or unnatural. Your instinct is to strike back, get even, make your abuser pay for what was done to you, or at least wish that your abuser suffers as much as you have. This can feel and appear to be empowering, and to be sure, for a time, your anger does make you strong and does put you back in charge of your life. However, as we have seen, anger eventually becomes a brittle power, easily breakable, and provides only a false sense of control.

> Blest are they who show mercy; mercy shall be theirs.
> —from Matthew 5:7

Forgiveness can also feel threatening. It can feel as if you are making yourself vulnerable to abuse once again. Forgiveness does involve eventually letting go of the anger at the abuser that you gained in the Anger Pathway. This holy anger helped you to feel empowered, free of shame and self-blame, your soul and your self once again sacred. So it may now appear to be insane and unsafe to let it go and forgive. Forgiveness is scary business, yet it is necessary business if you are to fully heal your heart, your mind, your soul, even your body. You cannot be fully free from your abuse unless you are open to forgiving your abuser.

Forgiveness does not mean that you are going soft and weak, are relinquishing your hard-won personal power. It does not mean that you will allow abuse back into your life. Forgiveness does not make you a victim again. In fact, as we shall see, through forgiveness, your soul empowers you for final victory over your abuse and your abuser. Forgiveness both comes from personal power and bestows and develops even greater personal power. As Mahatma Gandhi said, "The weak can never forgive. Forgiveness is the attribute of the strong."

As we have said, anger is vital for your healing, and yet it is meant to be a temporary path, not a place to remain indefinitely. Stuck anger, anger unresolved and unreleased, can turn into chronic bitter resentment that colors your whole persona and threatens to corrode your soul. Such anger directed inward could feed chronic depression and cause a certain numbness of spirit to impede your relationship with your soul. Chronic anger directed outwardly, coming from a deep reservoir of bitterness, is displayed in "flesh eating" (the literal Greek meaning of the word) sarcasm, or sarcastic humor, cynicism, a continually wary and critical spirit, defensiveness, and flashes of rage. Perhaps you know or have met someone with anger like this. They feel cold and prickly to be around, like a reptile version of the porcupine.

Remember the maxim: "Holding onto resentments is like swallowing the poison pill you intended for the one who hurt you." We saw in Part Four how necessary anger is for reconnecting to and re-empowering your soul, yet, held too long, anger turns into resentment and bitterness that poisons you. Eventually, you hurt not your offender, but yourself. Bitterness is like a cancer that invades your soul. If it is allowed to metastasize, it is you that suffers, not your abuser. Research has shown that chronic anger contributes to the development of a variety of physical and mental conditions. Researchers Frederic Luskin and Carl E. Thoresen, of Stanford's Forgiveness Project, have demonstrated a link between forgiveness and improved physical and emotional health, including a boost to your immune system. When you do not forgive, the person who pays the greater price is you, not your abuser. When you forgive, the person who receives the greatest gift is you.

Helen captures both the difficulty of forgiving abuse and the gift that it is for her, when she writes to her abuser:

> That day, you abused my body, but only bruised my spirit. The bruises do and did heal. It took time, but they have healed, at least all but one small one that is left. I've been told that forgiveness is the last step to healing that last bruise. I have known for a while that this day was coming. I am struggling with this concept of forgiving a person who hurt me in so many ways. I don't know how to forgive this, but if it is going to lead me to the freedom to love, and the ability to be a better minister, then I will try. I have come too far in this healing process not to consider forgiving you. Evil conquered your heart that day, but it does not have to conquer mine today.

Forgiveness is first of all for you. Forgiveness is primarily and first for the forgiver. Forgiveness is only secondarily for the abuser, for the one who offended you. The purpose of forgiveness is to set your soul free, to let it fly and soar. Chronic anger and bitterness ground your soul with heaviness and block your soul from fully expressing its love, its peace, and its desire for mercy. The beatitude about mercy reminds us of the circle of forgiveness: when you show mercy, you are blessed in turn with a merciful and loving heart for others and for yourself.

As I was writing this section, I decided to take a break and go for a walk on the grounds of the retreat center where I was staying. It was a rare sunny, late February day of the winter of 2010, a gloomy, unusually cold winter for Missouri and for much of the country. I stopped my walk at a small lake, soaking in the much-appreciated warmth of the sun that had finally appeared. When I was still for a moment, I was startled to hear a low, but clearly audible snap, crackle, and pop—like Rice Krispies in milk—coming somehow from the frozen, now-thawing lake surface. It took me a few moments of bewildered scanning and searching to notice that there were hundreds of tiny air bubbles being released from the ice as its surface melted in the warmth of the sun. This was the soft popping sound that I was hearing: air, oxygen, trapped in the cold ice, being set free.

I stood there for some time, simply enjoying the moment, looking down at the lake, and being present to the music of the thawing ice. Suddenly, I felt my soul and my gaze pulled upward and was thrilled to see seven or eight red tailed hawks, accompanied by two bald eagles, their white heads and tails gleaming in the sun, circling and soaring in the sky right above me. As my eyes adjusted to the brightness of the sun, I saw, too, that there was a faint, but rainbow-colorful arc of a sunbow above the sun that this raft of raptors were circling in and out of. I stood there for some time in awe, watching the hawks and eagles climb higher and higher in great, ascending spirals and then swiftly glide in twos and threes to the North, presumably and hopefully migrating towards an early spring.

> Forgiveness is the mightiest sword. Forgiveness of those you hate will be your highest reward.
>
> —from "Forgiveness," a song from *Jane Eyre: A Musical Drama* by Paul Gordon and John Caird

Creation sometimes gives me powerful symbols and metaphors. When I saw this scene, I felt like God had given me a sacramental moment to further illumine what anger, if held too long, does to the soul. Your anger, paradoxical to its fiery nature, when turned chronic and bitter, puts a hard, frozen shell around your soul. There is a certain cold pall over your heart that blocks the love and warmth that is at its center. There is soul life still going on under the ice—the fish are alive, if sluggish—and yet it is difficult for you to break though your frozen anger and to bring it forth from your soul to give to your self and to those around you that you want to love.

Choosing to forgive is the choice to thaw your frozen and soul chilling anger in the warmth of God's love. It releases life-giving spiritual oxygen, which bubbles back into your life with a snap, crackle and pop. It frees your soul to soar, gyre, and rise into new heights of life and freedom. Through your forgiveness, the Lord will raise you up to, as it says in Isaiah 40:31, "soar as with eagles' wings."

In her journal reflections for this chapter, Vickie expresses the powerful freeing effect of forgiveness as she describes her own forgiveness process and what it has changed for her. Remember, as Vicki describes so well, forgiveness is for you, for you to reclaim your soul in its fullness and light. Forgiveness is in your own enlightened self-interest. It is for your own healing. Forgiveness is a spiritual glue that helps you put your broken spirit back together again. This is forgiveness' first and primary spiritual purpose; forgiveness is only secondarily for those who abused you.

There is one other aspect of forgiving and letting go of anger that must be mentioned. Anger held too long actually binds you to your abuser. Anger keeps you chained to a negative relationship with your offender even if you have no contact with your abuser whatsoever. If you stay in anger at your abuser, you are continuing to give your abuser power over you. You stay tied to your abuser with the ropes and chains of anger, and you carry your abuser around with you every day. Forgiveness cuts these ties and breaks the abuse or trauma bond with your abuser for all time.

The final act of divorce is not contained in any legal document. The marriage is not truly over until the spouse chooses to forgive and release their ex-spouse to move on into a new and prayerfully happy life. Until then, the spouse remains unhappily married to their ex-spouse through their anger! So it can be with you and your abuser if you continue in anger past its time—no matter how justified the anger may be. In forgiving your abuser, you not only set your soul free; you finally, fully also set yourself free from your abuser and from any power your abuser may yet have over you. You break the chains of trauma that still tie you to your abuser. You drive your abuser out of your inner temple completely and eternally—now with the powerful sword of forgiveness.

It is important here to say clearly what forgiveness is not. Forgiveness of your abuser does not in any way excuse or condone what was done to you. In fact, forgiveness says to your abuser:

> *What you did to me was totally wrong and inexcusable. It was hurtful and damaging to me. Yet I no longer choose to stay in anger at you, and I surrender any desire to punish you or see you suffer. I pray, in fact, for your healing and for blessings on your life.*

Forgiveness does not necessarily mean that you cannot seek justice from your abuser if your soul so leads you.

Forgiveness is not denial. Forgiveness is not forgetting. You will never forget what was done to you. Nor should you. Forgiveness allows you to hold the memories of your abuse in your mind, heart, and soul, and yet be free to love, heal, and not be controlled by these painful memories. Forgiveness does not necessarily mean a restoration of your relationship with your abuser. Forgiveness and reconciliation with your offender are two different and distinct spiritual acts. Forgiveness may lead you to choose at some point to restore your relationship with your abuser, but it does not require such a choice. You can forgive and yet keep distant from your abuser; you can never have a relationship with your abuser again. For many survivors, this is the only sane and safe choice. A relationship with their abuser would be too toxic or even spiritually, emotionally, or physically dangerous. Your soul calls you to forgive and yet also cries out for you to never again put yourself in a place of abuse.

Forgiveness, as powerfully healing as it can be, is a very daunting and difficult spiritual task, especially in regard to forgiving someone who has hurt you so deeply through abuse. It is also a process that must ripen in soul time, in the fullness of God's time. Such forgiveness is a process that unfolds in you. It is not usually a single, one-time choice to forgive. Its timing, duration, and progression is different for each survivor. Give yourself whatever time and space you need on the Forgiveness Pathway.

It is, in fact, vital to walk the Forgiveness Pathway slowly. Quick forgiveness is usually false or phony forgiveness. What you forgive prematurely or too freely, or under guilt or compulsion, does not stay forgiven. To genuinely forgive, you need first to have thoroughly traveled the Anger and Grief Pathways. To forgive, you must allow yourself your anger at your abuser and have felt and grieved the pain your abuser has caused you. Sometimes, too, forgiveness is like peeling the layers of an onion: each time you choose to forgive and surrender your anger, another layer is revealed for the next step in your forgiveness journey.

So be gentle and patient with yourself. Do not heap guilt on yourself about wherever you happen to be in the forgiveness process or about how much time it takes you to forgive. Forgiveness is not meant to be another "should" to beat or berate your self with. Your soul is eternal and eternally patient with you.

Ultimately, too, forgiveness is a matter of grace. Forgiveness for such awful trauma and harm is beyond your capacity to choose and give by your power alone. Yet, grace from God and your soul is there for the asking. All that is required of you to begin your travel on the Forgiveness Pathway is to choose to ask for the grace to forgive and to be willing to receive it. Or, if even that is too daunting, it is enough, as it is sometimes said, to be willing, to be willing, to be willing…to begin to forgive.

 *Way Station*

🖋 Reflect and pray about this section that you have just read.
   Ask yourself where you are in the forgiveness process:

Are you at the very start of the Forgiveness Pathway?

Are you willing to be willing to ask for the grace to forgive?

Or are you farther down the path and almost ready to surrender all of your no-longer-needed anger?

What is the next step for you on the Forgiveness Pathway, and what will you need from your soul and from God to make this step?

🖋 Prayerfully consider exactly who, what, and why you want to forgive. In addition to your abuser, you may want to forgive others in some way connected to your abuse. It is important to explore your motivation to forgive. Does it come from a genuine readiness and desire to surrender your hurt and anger, or do you feel compelled or guilty?

🖋 If you are ready, begin to write a letter of forgiveness in your journal. Write it to your abuser or abusers, but do not send it. Take your time with this. Make sure you are ready to write so that your words will come from your heart. Ask God or your soul to give you the grace, the words, and the courage to do this.

🖋 Do the Walking Meditation again, this time from the Forgiveness Pathway. In your backpack, put your anger at your abuser and whatever readiness or willingness to forgive that you possess at this point in your journey. Bring it to the top of the mountain and your encounter with the spiritual being you meet there. Unpack your anger and your current openness to forgive in the presence of the spiritual being. Be aware of what you hear, see, and feel as you do so. Later, in your journal, record what you experience .

Journal

Forgiveness is first for you, the survivor. Vicki here relates the emotional and spiritual cost of not moving in time toward forgiveness and the spiritual power and freedom of the difficult, but vital choice to forgive.

From Vicki's Journal—

I lived the terrible pain of unforgiveness for so long. It ground away at me in the grinding of my teeth, the clenched fists of my hands, the nerves that often felt frayed, the inability to sleep, the endless hours of work I used to bury my feelings, and the occasional violent thoughts that clouded my perception of reality. As I grew, I came to learn that nothing good comes from holding persistent anger and hatred—that over-riding sense of unforgiveness. There is no clearer message in the Gospels than to forgive one another. Being unable to forgive eats away at your soul, and if we cannot come to for-

giveness, all we are left with is the pain that unforgiveness leaves. The grace that opens our hearts to forgiveness comes when we acknowledge our powerlessness in changing that which we cannot forgive.

I liken it to those who seek capital punishment. They somehow hold the belief that the death of the one who took their loved one away from them is going to bring them the peace they seek. It does not. Instead, it solidifies their sense of unforgiveness, and then it is allowed to invade their persona the rest of their lives. I made a conscious decision to forgive my abuser and to live the life I have been given. It wasn't the life I would have chosen for myself; however, it is the life I have embraced wholeheartedly. It is a radical forgiveness that Jesus calls each of us to embrace. And nothing about this is easy.

There was a great sense of relief at finally letting go of my anger and saying with gusto, "I forgive my abuser!" I want to carry within me that which gives life and love. In death, I give him the peace of a life well lived. My prayer for those who are stuck in that persistent state of unforgiveness is that they can know peace when they surrender the hate and anguish in their soul and bathe in the fecundity of understanding and love. I believe I am called to live a life of gracious forgiveness just as I seek the same from those in my own life. I feel I am free to live this on a daily basis today.

A friend recently shared a visual reflection on living a non-violent way of life. It is called the "Two Hands of Non-Violence." As she spoke this to me and demonstrated it for me, it resonated profoundly. This is the stance I wish to hold in my heart, and this has helped me to embrace the forgiveness of my abuser in a more genuine way. And it has helped me to take a different stance with the institutional church. It is centered in the acknowledgement that we are all broken in some way: (Adapted from Barbara Deming, Revolution and Equilibrium, New York: Grossman Publishers, 1971)

With one hand (in stop position, elbow bent, palm facing forward) I say, "Stop what you are doing. You may not abuse me. You may not oppress me. I refuse to obey you. I refuse to cooperate with your demands. I refuse to build the walls and the bombs. I refuse to pay for the guns. I will even interfere with the wrong you are doing. I will not submit to this injustice, not merely because it is destroying me, but because it is destroying you as well."

With the other hand (outstretched, maybe with love and sympathy, maybe not, but always outstretched, elbow bent, palm up) I say, "I won't let go of you or cast you out of the circle of my care and concern. I have faith that you can make a better choice than you are making now, and I'll be here when you are ready. Like it or not, we are part of one another, part of the beloved community, part of the sacred web of creation."

It has taken a long time for me to say the words, "I forgive my abuser." He died in 2002. I had the opportunity to visit him on his deathbed, but chose not to see him. I feared nothing had changed in him, and so I chose instead to protect myself. I protected the hard work I had accomplished in rebuilding my self-esteem. I question that decision often, wondering if I should have given him a chance to say some healing word. If I had known the "Two Hands" non-violent prayer then, perhaps I would have had a different courage.

Not long after his death, I did feel a release of sorts, and greater clarity emerged, a clarity that allowed me to see my abuser in a different light. I could see him as a wounded man, someone who had lost his wife less than a year after they were married. I could see, finally, that perhaps he had never healed from this tremendous loss in his life, so all he had left to do was transmit this pain to others. I was aware that my self-righteousness had lessened, and I could, for the first time, acknowledge the good things he had done in his life. He touched the lives of many people through his work and ministry. In my association with him, I honed my own leadership style that has stayed with me all these years. He inspired a missionary heart in me, and for that I shall be grateful forever. And he sexually abused me for fourteen years. Now I can see the gift and the hurt apart from each other and see both aspects of his life. I will never know if he was able to acknowledge this abusive part of his life, but I don't really need to know now.

19

Forgiveness as Spiritual Revolution

Forgiveness, for so great a harm as abuse, both requires and creates a spiritual revolution in the forgiver. Forgiveness needs the grace of a complete turnaround, an overthrowing of what your ego, sometimes called your lower self, wants when you have been abused. In turn, the choice and act of forgiveness turns you around, moves you from your old self, and lifts you up further into your new higher self. This is the spiritual revolution that your soul desires for you in calling you to forgiveness.

Metanoia is the Greek biblical name for spiritual revolution. It is often inadequately translated as "repentance," but it means much more than that. The word comes from *meta* which means "beyond or after," and *nous*, which means "mind"—literally "beyond mind." *Metanoia* captures the sense of what is necessary for, and also results from, your forgiveness: a transformational change of your mind, heart, and spirit concerning your abuse, your abuser, and your self—a spiritual revolution and rebirth.

> Peter came up and asked him, "Lord, when my brother wrongs me, how often must I forgive him? Seven Times?" "No", Jesus replied, "not seven times; I say, seventy times seven times."
> —from Matthew 18:21-22

A conversional paradigm shift is another way to describe the grace needed for the forgiveness of abuse and the grace that is given by forgiveness. A paradigm shift is an in-depth change in or basic re-orientation of your central paradigm, your way of seeing the world based on your inner beliefs and perceptions about your self, your abuse, and your life. A paradigm shift leads to a profound and lasting change of core attitudes, choices, and behaviors. The *metanoiac* paradigm shift of forgiveness means creating and repeatedly telling yourself a new story, a new narrative, about your abuse and your abuser. This opens up new consciousness, awareness, and healing.

Sue gives us a good example in her journal reflections of just such a *metanoia* and transformational paradigm shift. Sue was sexually molested by a Catholic priest at age four. As a therapist, she has counseled hundreds of women who have been abused. She is very aware of the great damage that abuse has done to her and to her clients. So when she and I were invited to co-lead a group for priests and brothers who have abused minors, Sue confronted her hatred for perpetrators of abuse. Her story describes her process of forgiving her abuser, and this group of abusers, so that she could answer her soul's call to work with these men to aid in their healing. Through forgiveness, her hate was transformed to a deep love for each and every man in the group. This is the revolutionary *metanoia* of forgiveness.

The paradigm change of forgiveness is different for different survivors. Let's look now at some of the most common changes that we see in our clients as they go through the process of forgiveness. One of the key paradigm shifts that we first explored in Chapter Nine is from victim, to survivor, to thriver, a process that is part of each of the pathways and which continues and speeds up on the Forgiveness Pathway.

The shift to the thriver paradigm involves several changes and realizations. Oprah Winfrey, herself a survivor of childhood sexual abuse, once defined forgiveness as the ability "to accept the fact that the past can't change." We don't get do-overs in life, no matter how deserved they may be. Accepting this as part of the forgiveness process can free you from holding onto and obsessing over your grievance story about the past. You come to the awareness that what is really hurting you now is not the abuse itself. It is you, holding onto your anger and pain, and holding your anger and pain against your abuser. You cannot change the past. You can, however, change your relationship to the past and to the abuse itself.

> To forgive is to set a prisoner free and discover that the prisoner was you.
> —from Lewis B. Smedes's article "Forgiveness—The Power to Change the Past"

Forgiveness is the key to changing this relationship. Forgiveness includes the consciousness that you no longer need your grievance story, the willingness to surrender it to your soul or the God of your understanding, and the courage to amend your grievance story with the heroic power to forgive. This frees you from staying a victim to your grievance story. It frees you from believing that you are only capable, because of the abuse, of merely surviving and getting by. It creates a new paradigm for you that moves you into the thriver zone of your recovery. You can now see that you are not captive to the past, nor merely surviving your abuse. You have the power to let go of the past and no longer live there. You have the strength to forgive and so to shed the burdens of carrying your abuse and your abuser like a sack of radioactive rocks strapped to your back.

A powerful part of the paradigm shift of the forgiveness revolution is recognizing that you can and do create your own reality, even about your abuse and your abuser. Remember my observation that 90% of what makes us happy about our lives is not the events or circumstances of our lives. Rather, happiness comes from how we look at our lives. Happiness, or unhappiness, is our set of attitudes, perceptions, and beliefs about ourselves and our lives. To a large degree, we create our own reality, and also how we feel about that reality, even if we have experienced serious life traumas. When you were young and under the power of your abuser, your abuser controlled and shaped your reality to one degree or another. Part of the healing process of these pathways has involved you taking back and re-shaping your own reality. Forgiveness requires and potentiates another leap forward in this reality-defining process. Unforgiveness keeps you in the old reality of the abuse, and, as we have seen, in the reality defined by your abuser. Forgiveness is the act in which you reclaim the power to shape your own reality and carry it forward it into the present moment.

Another major paradigm shift involved in forgiveness is seeing your abuser in a new light, illuminated by your soul. This is a shift from seeing your abuser, and abuse perpetrators in general, as evil or monstrous to seeing them as wounded, sick, and often addicted. They are wounded as you are wounded. Their wounding of you arose from their own wounds. This is the tragic cycle of abuse. It is one of the main lessons Sue and I learned as we moved from working primarily with survivors of abuse to also counseling perpetrators. This is one of the primary messages of our previous book, *Broken Trust*. Listening to the stories of abusers in counseling, and seeing how their abusive behavior very often began in their own experience of childhood abuse, put them in a whole different light for us.

Research supports this view. In *Broken Trust*, we reported that some studies have shown that 62-81% of sex offenders were sexually abused as children or adolescents; other studies suggest that 97% of sexual abusers were themselves sexually, physically, or severely emotionally abused during their youth. This does not mean that your abuser's actions are justified or excused by his sickness or his abuse history. It does not make the damage he did to you any less hurtful. It does, however, invite you to a change of heart, a *metanoia*, in regard to how you view your abuser, and this change of heart opens the door to self-healing forgiveness.

Consciousness of seeing your abuser in this changed way brings another paradigm shift. Victims understandably tend to view their abuse and their abuser as an us-versus-them scenario. This is actually a necessary phase in the healing process, especially as you empower yourself with your anger to protect yourself from further abuse and heal from shame. The spiritual revolution of the Forgiveness Pathway now challenges you, though, to move from the us-versus-them paradigm to seeing your abuser as a fellow sufferer, caught together with you in the vicious cycle of abuse. You are not enemies. You are brothers and sisters struggling with the same great burden and wound of abuse. This paradigm has the potential to break open your heart and soul to a whole new vision of your abuse and your abuser. It opens your heart to forgiveness and much more.

The willingness to forgive is a powerful spiritual sword and the seedbed for a revolution of soul in regard to your abuse. It is a liberating path out of victimhood and a victory of soul over the harm that your abuser has caused you. Forgiveness completes your healing from shame and fear and opens your heart to deeper self-acceptance and self-love. Through forgiveness, the past is no longer the primary focus of your mind. Your heart and soul can now be more mindful of the gifts of the present moment and the possibilities of the future.

Becky asks for the grace of forgiveness and healing, and captures the spirit of the transformational power of forgiveness in one of her poems about her healing journey:

> *I come to You*
> *broken and bruised,*
> *sad and confused.*
> *I need to be healed.*
> *You are the only true healer of my wounded soul.*
> *Extend your Divine Hands*
> *To reach a heart*
> *Immobilized by*
> *anger,*
> *lies,*
> *fears,*
> *worthlessness,*
> *and guilt.*
> *Allow them to rest upon my head,*
> *and redefine the line that separates*
> *justifiability from excuses,*
> *and morals from selfishness.*
> *Pierce my gloom with the Radiance of Your Light*
> *And grace me with the compassion needed*
> *to forgive myself and my abusers,*
> *and the strength*
> *to let go of that*
> *which encumbers me.*

 ## Way Station

Reflect and pray on this section in your journal, especially on these questions:

What change or *metanoia* is needed in you to move forward towards forgiveness of your abuser?

What encumbers you, or what blocks you from choosing to forgive?

What will your spiritual revolution of forgiveness look like for you?

How will forgiveness of your abuser change you? What *metanoia* will it create in you?

What core paradigms or life perceptions will forgiveness shift or transform in you?

Write a prayer in your journal asking your soul, or God, for the change of heart needed to be willing to forgive.

Ask your soul to imagine or discover an object, image, or other symbol that would represent the spirit of forgiveness for you. Once you have found it, place it in some prominent position in your living space so that you will see it each day. Pray on its meaning for you.

20

Forgiveness Re-humanizes the Abused and the Abuser

In every act of abuse, both the victim and the abuser are de-humanized and objectified. In your abuse, your abuser used you as an object of lust, anger, or power. You were used to meet your abuser's sick, wounded, ego-driven, often compulsive needs. In the act of abuse, you became a non-person without your own feelings, needs, and rights to love and freedom. This is the demeaning and dehumanizing experience forced on the victim of abuse.

What may surprise you is that a similar thing happens to abusers in the act of abuse. They too are dehumanized and objectified by their own illness and actions. Listening to our clients who have abused describe their own experience of abusing, it has become clear to us that they too become vehicles and objects of the sickness that infected them, took control of them, and led them to abuse. Their act of abuse, driven by their woundedness, de-humanizes them, numbing and at least temporarily paralyzing their capacity for human feeling, empathy, compassion, conscience, and rationality. Abusers, too, become objects and non-persons in the act of abusing.

Forgiveness heals this objectification on both sides of abuse, and helps to restore the sacred personhood of both victim and abuser. When you let your soul guide you to a new vision of your abuser in the forgiveness process, you will be empowered to develop a compassionate understanding and empathy for your

> If only there were evil people somewhere insidiously committing evil deeds, and it were necessary only to separate them from the rest of us and destroy them. But the line dividing good and evil cuts through the heart of every human being. And who is willing to destroy a piece of his own heart?
> —from Aleksandr I. Solzhenitsyn's *Gulag Archipelago*

abuser's story and perhaps for your abuser himself. As mentioned in the last section, this is quite difficult, yet possible with the *metanoia* and grace that comes from being willing to forgive.

Again, this does not mean that you excuse what was done to you. Rather, you begin to see the wounded, human person behind the abusive behavior. Your openness to forgive brings a compassionate understanding of your abuser's story that reveals the shared, wounded humanity of your abuser. You start to see that your abuser is a fellow suffering brother or sister with a wounded heart and broken spirit akin to yours, caught like you in the cycle of abuse, and so too rendered a non-person by abuse. Forgiveness, accompanied by this compassionate, spiritual understanding, sets both you and your abuser free from the dehumanizing, objectifying power of abuse. You may even come to the place, like Sue, where you can love—whatever that means to you—your abuser, while still always hating what your abuser did to you. Or, to use an old spiritual aphorism, you will be led by your soul to "hate the sin, and love the sinner."

In my experience, when you know someone's story, it puts them and their actions in a whole new light. It becomes much more difficult to judge, condemn, or demonize them. Sue and I have been privileged to hear many hundreds of sacred stories of the abused and of the perpetrators of abuse. When you hear a person's sacred story, you begin to see the light of their soul emerging from the dark shadow of their woundedness and illness. You feel the bond of your shared, if wounded and limited, humanity. At this stage of your healing, if you could hear or know your abuser's own story of abuse and pain, I believe that you would experience what we have experienced.

This why the healing heart of our book, *Broken Trust*, is the stories, in their own words, of Catholic priests who have abused, as well as of victims who have healed. The abusers' stories illustrate how their own childhood experiences of various kinds of abuse wounded them and infected them with a sickness that in them (the greater majority of victims of abuse do not go on to abuse) gradually led to becoming abusers in return. We helped these men tell their stories and express their apologies for their abusive actions so that survivors could understand that their abuse did not happen because of something wrong in them and also to aid survivors in the healing process of forgiveness. Our hope and prayer is that these stories will help create an indirect dialogue between abuser and victim that could open up compassionate understanding leading to forgiveness and healing.

The Forgiveness Pathway can help you re-humanize your abuser, and, in doing so, continue to de-objectify yourself. It empowers you to see your abuser as a human being, wounded and suffering, even as he unjustly passes on that suffering to you. It also allows you to see the possibility that your abuser can and might have changed as well as how your abuser is suffering now. Unforgiveness freezes both you and your abuser in the past. You are frozen with your abuser in the moment of abuse. Forgiveness and compassionate understanding gifts you with the possibility of seeing your abuser in the present, as he or she is now. In our experience, some abusers never acknowledge their abusive actions, and remain engulfed in and swallowed up by the darkness of their sickness. Some abusers, however, especially those who have engaged in extensive treatment, do emerge from their denial and the control of their sickness and can become relatively healthy in their recovery. They feel great shame and sorrow for what they have done to their victims. If given the opportunity, they want to apologize to their victims and make whatever amends is possible. They live with a great weight of pain about the damage they have done.

You may or you may not know your own abuser's story. It might be possible for you to find out from other family members how your abuser became what he became and did what he did to you. Sometimes there is a way open to this, and sometimes there is not. This pathway may be a time for you to attempt to find out about your abuser's story and come to some understanding. It is important that, in doing this, you do not re-expose yourself to further abuse of any kind, so be wise as you pursue this. If the way to discovering the story is closed or unsafe, there are other options. You can either use your imagination and whatever facts you do know to construct a story of your abuser, or you can read and adopt one of the stories in *Broken Trust* or elsewhere, as a surrogate story for your abuser.

> If one can understand why people behave as they do, then often the road to forgiveness is opened.
>
> —from Terry Waite, held hostage for five years by terrorists in Lebanon, on Forgiveness Project.com

To aid you in this, I want to briefly tell you two other stories of clerical sexual abusers that Sue and I have worked with and relay their letters of apology to their victims in their own words. Perhaps, in hearing their story, you may be able to understand your own abuser's story. Perhaps you can receive their apology to their victims somehow as an apology to yourself for what was done to you. Your soul will open you to whatever is most healing for you.

The first is "Bob's" story. Bob was sexually assaulted by a group of other boys when he was eleven and just starting a new school. He never told anyone of this abuse, or got any help to deal with it. A deep inner anger, shame, and hidden darkness grew in Bob through the rest of his childhood and adolescence because of this assault. As a young man, Bob volunteered as a lay missionary in a remote foreign country. He was eventually ordained as a Catholic missionary with the intent of spending his whole life in the missions in the service of the people of his adopted land. His plans were derailed when he and his people became embroiled in a tragic and violent civil war. Bob was very traumatized by this experience, by the violence he witnessed, by the threats that were directed at him, and by having to flee the country in fear of his life. He returned to parish work in the United States with symptoms of PTSD. Again, he did not seek help, and instead, he threw himself into his new pastoral work to the extent of becoming a severe workaholic. A few years later, he began to physically and sexually abuse teenage boys.

Bob felt relieved when he was caught and arrested. He pleaded guilty, was sent to intensive inpatient treatment, and was eventually sent on probation to the supervised recovery residence where Sue and I provide counseling. He will be there for the rest of his life. Bob fully entered into a recovery and healing process, taking complete responsibility for his abusive actions, while establishing a personal recovery and safety program and working to heal his own trauma from which his abuse arose.

Bob cooperated with both the criminal trial and civil suits resulting from his abuse with the intention of helping his victims heal through this process as well as possible. He often silently prayed for his victims as he heard their testimony against him. He lives daily with the awareness and pain of what he did to his victims and the damage that he caused them. He prays for his victims and for their healing each day. He now sees his ministerial mission is to serve his fellow priests and brothers in the recovery community where he resides. This is Bob's apology letter to his victims:

> I am so deeply sorry for the abuse and pain that I caused you.
> You came to me with the belief that I was a good person. You trusted me to guide you. And I lied to you about who I am. I will never know how deeply I hurt you by using that trust to abuse you.
> You could not know that you were placing your life in the hands of a person with extreme mental illness. I will live the rest of my life in a recovery facility that will keep me from other people so that I cannot hurt anyone else.
> There is no way I can give you back what I have taken from you. You have every reason to hate me. All I can do is hope God will help you to leave behind the damage that I caused so that you can live your life in peace.

The second story is "Tom's." His story is one of the most tragic and dramatically illustrative examples of the full cycle of abuse that I have ever encountered. Tom's father verbally, emotionally, and physically abused Tom through his whole childhood. At times, the abuse was brutal. On at least one occasion, his father almost killed Tom in a blind rage. Tom grew up to be a wounded little boy in a man's body. He sought love and approval wherever he could find it, in a variety of inappropriate and unhealthy ways.

Eventually, Tom became an ordained priest and worked in parish ministry. During a time of great personal emotional and spiritual stress and turmoil, Tom met a very hurting and needy twelve-year-old boy from the parish. Tom reached

out to the boy with the conscious intent of helping him. What his unconscious-
ness purpose was, Tom did not know at the time. One day when they were
alone in the rectory—a fatal mistake—the boy asked Tom to hold him. The
holding became sexual. Later, Tom learned that the boy's uncle was also abusing him sexually. The boy was already a victim! Tragically, instead of helping the
boy, being a responsible adult and a caring priest, Tom abused him and continued the circle of abuse that the boy was already caught in. Something of Tom's
own woundedness and abuse was triggered in him, and so Tom initiated further
sexual abuse on a few other occasions, and then stopped the abuse on his own.

Tom held this secret inside for many years. Over time, he got professional
help and healing for at least some of his own abuse history, but he was terrified
to admit to anyone that he had abused this boy. Finally, thankfully, his victim
came forward, broke the silence, and accused Tom of the abuse. Tom admit-
ted it, confessed, and finally sought treatment. He was eventually sentenced to
prison, serving time for his crime just as his victim did, since that young man
tragically went on to sexually abuse another young victim, continuing the vicious cycle of abuse.

This is Tom's apology letter to his victim:

> *To the victim that I sexually abused many years ago,*
>
> *I wish that I could say to you face-to-face how sorry I am for the
> pain and hurt that I caused you, but the legal system will not allow me
> to do this. So I am writing this letter to you and to all victims of sexual
> abusers. I apologize to you from the depths of my heart and soul for your
> pain and hurt.*
>
> *Every day, I lift you, my victim, up to God for your pain and hurt,
> and I ask God to watch over you and protect you. I have been in therapy
> for almost two years, and soon I will be going to trial to pay for what I
> have done to you. I take full responsibility for my actions back then and
> accept whatever is dealt to me by the court system. I am responsible and
> accountable for what I have done to you.*
>
> *The realization I have now of the enormity of the guilt, shame, and
> hurt that I caused you, my victim, has become unbearable, but everyday
> I ask God for the strength to see me through the day, and He has done
> this for me. If God can do this for me the abuser, He can do the same for
> you victims. I pray that you allow God to heal your pain and hurt. God
> wants this for you. Again, I apologize for what I have done to you, fully
> and painfully understanding that these words cannot undo the harm
> that I caused you.*
>
> *Thank you,*
> *your abuser*

Way Station

 Having read the two stories of abusers in this section, and their apology letters, what do you feel inside? What do you hear your soul saying to you about them? Reflect on this in your journal.

 Take some time to gather whatever information is available to you about your abuser's story. If necessary, use your imagination to fill in the gaps in the story. Your intuitive imagination will likely capture the spirit of your abuser's story, whether or not the details are accurate. Then write your abuser's story in your journal. After you have written it, take time to pray or meditate over the story. Look at it from various viewpoints: your viewpoint as a survivor, your abuser's viewpoint, your soul's perspective. Notice what you come to feel about your abuser's story. Be aware of what you feel now towards your abuser. Has anything shifted or changed?

 Do the Walking Meditation once again from the Forgiveness Pathway, beginning at the ocean and beach. This time, as you begin to climb the mountain trail, you will notice that there is a figure off in the distance who is on a separate trail ascending the mountain. It is your abuser. Do not be afraid. You are safe. Your abuser's path is different than yours, and a large chasm lies between the two trails. When you reach the top of the mountain, as usual, you are greeted by a spiritual being. After spending some time with this being, you notice that your abuser is sitting on a rock below you, again at a safe distance, on the other side of a deep canyon. Your abuser cannot see you. Only you and the spiritual being can see your abuser. Contemplating this scene, be aware of what you feel deep inside as you behold your abuser. How does your soul view this encounter with your abuser? How does the spiritual being look upon your abuser? When your time on the mountaintop is complete, return down the mountain, through the forest to the beach as you have in the past. Your abuser descends by the separated path, and you do not see him again. Record your experience in your journal.

Journal

It may be unimaginable for you to envision ever forgiving your abuser or the person responsible for your trauma. With grace and openness to the leading of your soul, it is possible. You will be surprised at the new awareness and feeling that will come. In this journal entry, Sue describes her moment of forgiveness of her abuser and the new light that it shone on him in her eyes.

From Sue's Journal—

All healing is a process. The forgiveness part of healing is a process as well. God's love brings up everything unlike itself for the purpose of healing. This comes in God's time when the moment is fully ripe for healing and forgiveness. I had an unusual experience of this just a year and a half ago. I was speaking at a workshop Pat, Vicki, and I were doing in San Francisco on these Pathways. We were presenting to a national conference of Victim Assistance Coordinators, a wonderful group of people dedicated to aid in the healing process of victims of abuse by Catholic clergy. I was standing at the podium speaking about the healing power of forgiveness when I suddenly experienced a strange sensation in my body and then a fleeting picture of my mother being sexually assaulted by Monsignor. I have learned to listen to my body and to honor the sacredness of these experiences. I listened to what was happening within me while continuing to present the planned material. Then it really hit me. I had never actually forgiven the priest for molesting my mom and me and for the horrendous toll the effects of my mom's abuse took on our family, and here I was talking on forgiveness!

I stopped my talk. I took a few deep breaths and shared with the audience what was going on within me at that moment. This broke all my fear rules because, in doing so, I allowed my self to be visible and to have a voice. I acknowledged to the group that I had not yet forgiven Monsignor and then chose right there and then to forgive him with the group of sixty or so people as my witnesses. I felt a momentary wave of release and lightness and was ready to go on with my part of the workshop.

When I reflected on this experience later, I realized that I had probably been ready to forgive Monsignor for some time. It was sitting on the shelf, so to speak. I had just not picked it up and looked at it until that moment in time. This choice to forgive Monsignor was the last major piece of the puzzle of my healing process. Much healing had already occurred, and now this piece freed me further to lay the past to rest and be mostly done with it.

A large part of what brought me to this point of forgiveness was my therapeutic work and personal experience with the priests and brothers of the residential recovery program where Pat and I provide counseling. Listening with sacred listening to their sacred stories of their own abuse and hearing their commitment to healing and recovery for themselves and for their victims had opened my heart, mind, and soul to a new vision of perpetrators of abuse. I could see the woundedness that had spawned their abusive behavior. I could see the sickness and suffering that was behind their abusive actions. I could see their desire to be spiritually free and whole. What they wanted was the same thing that I wanted for myself and for all of my other clients who had been abused.

This experience with these men had led me to wonder about Monsignor's sacred story. What abuse or other trauma had led him to do the awful things that he did to my mother and me? What sickness had created these behaviors? He clearly suffered from alcoholism. What great pain he must have been in with this sickness and with whatever sexual sickness he also was gripped by. What did he feel in his lucid moments when he realized what he and his priesthood had come to? How awful it must have been for him to be so out of control, and to be living in such total contradiction to his calling. Hearing the stories of the men that we counsel had revealed to me the inner world of intense suffering that many perpetrators experience at the core of their intense and out-of-control sickness. This had led me to see Monsignor with a spiritual vision that had opened my heart to forgive him that day in San Francisco. Sadly, I very much doubt that Monsignor ever got any help, care, or healing from his sickness as a perpetrator. Tragically, this parallels my mother's life. Neither ever received the healing help that could have set them both free.

21

Forgiveness Breaks the Cycle of Abuse

I have been blessed with many deeply spiritual moments in my career as therapist: when the scales of hurt and fear fall from a couple's eyes, they see each other again, and their love is rekindled; when the veil of shame finally falls away from an abuse survivor, and they begin to love and accept themselves and know their goodness; when an addict first begins to realize the blessings and freedom of recovery, and this becomes stronger than the pull back to the addiction. One of the most sacred experiences I have had as therapist was when I facilitated a meeting between an abusive priest and one of his victims. This priest was then in his late seventies. He had sexually abused several young girls over a number of years while serving in various pastoral positions. He finally stopped when he was caught and sent to prison for another sexual offense. He was grateful that he was caught and punished since it brought his terrible abusive behavior to a complete end. This occurred over thirty years prior to his coming into counseling with me. His full story can be found in *Broken Trust*.

Pain that is not transformed is transmitted.
—from Richard Rohr's *How Do We Breathe Under Water?*

He had been in counseling with me for a little over a year when one of his victims called and asked for a meeting with him. She was by then a woman in her early fifties. They both agreed that it would be helpful if I was present for the meeting. The aged priest began the meeting in my office by again apologizing to his victim (they had met once before) for abusing her and for the tremendous harm he had caused her. She accepted his apology and then expressed her forgiveness and her concern for his well-being. He was able to answer some questions about the past that she felt would be helpful for her healing. I was able to explain to her some aspects of his history and sickness that we had discovered in the counseling that I thought would also help in her healing. One of the most moving moments came when I told her that the priest had also been sexually abused when he was a child. This was information that the priest had revealed to me for the first time just a few months prior to the meeting. He had never told anyone before. She appeared to be deeply saddened to hear that he too had been abused and said to the priest how sorry she was for him.

It is difficult to put into words the feeling that was in that room as we spoke. There was the sense of a sacred moment. There was a felt presence of divine Spirit. There was a holy and palpable peace. It felt, too, that a great weight of pain had been lifted from all of us, and an old and rusty chain had been broken and carried away. I later reflected that it was as if the awful Gordian knot of abuse had been cut by the priest's apology and by the woman's forgiveness and compassion for his story. They had together broken the cycle of abuse.

Sadly, these very healing apology and forgiveness meetings are rare in my experience. A number of factors intervene: the abuser is sometimes unwilling to acknowledge the abuse; it is not emotionally or physically safe for the victim to meet with the abuser; or family or legal considerations make such a meeting difficult or impossible. If such a meeting is not possible for you, there is still much you can do to experience the healing of forgiveness. By forgiving your abuser, whether in person or not, you can cut the Gordian knot that binds you to the abuse, and, in doing so, you can break the cycle of abuse for yourself and your family. You can end it now with you, so that it is not passed on to the next generation.

Richard Rohr's words at the head of this chapter are tragically true. The pain you do not transform, you will unwittingly, unconsciously, and in some fashion transmit or pass on to your children, your life partners, your family, your friends, even your spiritual community, your workplace, and your coworkers. Perhaps this is the core wisdom of the traditional Christian concept of original sin. How you transmit your pain will differ from survivor to survivor, but, sadly, unless you heal and release your pain, you will indeed convey it to those you love. And the cycle of abuse will keep going round and round.

Part of our hope and prayer is that these pathways will give you the tools and healing experiences to stop this destructive wheel from turning in your life and in your world. Hurting people hurt. Wounded people wound. Again, though, the cycle can stop with you. It is your soul's desire that you do so. Forgiveness is one of the most powerful tools you can use to transform your abuse wounds and pain and prevent you from spreading your pain to those you love.

Forgiveness is also one of the most powerful tools you can use to transform your relationship with God. Some survivors find it necessary and liberating to include forgiving God in their forgiveness process. As I mentioned earlier in the book, many survivors feel abandoned and rejected by God because of trauma or abuse. They struggle with the questions: Where was God when the abuse happened? Why didn't God stop the abuse, and protect me better? If you share these feelings, and especially if they have become major blocks in your spiritual growth and healing, you may want to work on forgiving God. You may think it is silly, disrespectful, or even grandly presumptuous to be forgiving the Creator of the Universe, yet I believe that it is a mark of deep respect and reverence. It can also be very a freeing and peace-yielding release of any anger you have held against God concerning your abuse.

This section brings up the question of whether or not to meet with your abuser. This is a difficult and delicate issue, which yields a different answer and solution for each survivor. Some survivors find it necessary to meet with their abusers and at least confront them with their responsibility for the abuse and its effects. Some do not find this required for their healing. Some speak their forgiveness in person to their abusers. Some express it to their abusers in the Spirit through writing, visualization, or meditation. It is up to you to discern what fits for you. Your soul will guide you.

There are some important things to consider in your discernment. I believe that it is generally advisable not to confront your abuser until you are some place in the forgiveness process and your justifiable anger at your abuser is under your control. My concern is that your anger might lead you to you say or do something that might be harmful or destructive for you. Expressing your anger directly to your abuser can be very empowering and healing, but it will be more so if it comes from a healed spirit within you. You must also be prepared for the very real possibility that your abuser will not admit to or apologize for the abuse. This can be very hurtful, and so it is, I have found, better that your healing is solid and far-progressed before you confront.

Do not meet with your abuser alone. It is highly advisable that you have a therapist present to guide and facilitate such a meeting. Ideally, the therapist will meet with both of you ahead of time to assess both sides' readiness for the meeting and to ensure the most healing interaction possible. Many survivors have also found it reassuring and healing to have one of their soul friends present for support and witness.

The other option is, as mentioned, to confront and forgive your abuser in an imagined meeting through spiritual visualization or role-play. There is one

> It's forgiveness that makes us what we are. Without forgiveness, our species would have annihilated itself in endless retribution. Without forgiveness there would be no history. Without that hope, there would be no art, for every work of art is in some way an act of forgiveness. Without that dream, there would be no love, for every act of love is in some way a promise to forgive. We live on because we can love, and we love because we can forgive.
>
> —from Gregory David Roberts's *Shamtaram*

possible method outlined in the Way Station. This can be equally powerful and liberating as an in-person encounter. It has the advantage of being emotionally—and sometimes physically—safer. It is particularly indicated when there is a safety issue or when it is likely that your abuser will not admit the abuse or apologize for it. In the realm of Spirit and soul, if you forgive your abuser, whether physically present or not, it is done. The relationship between the two of you is cleared. The knot that bound you to your abuser is cut. The cycle of abuse is broken. You and, in some spiritual sense, your abuser are set free.

 ## *Way Station*

One way to implement forgiveness is to go on what the spiritual writer, Sondra Ray, calls the "Forgiveness Diet." It involves creating forgiveness affirmations such as:

> *I am willing to be, to be willing, to be willing…to forgive my abuser.*
> *I forgive you, (name), my abuser.*
> *I forgive you, (name), I bless you, and I set you free.*
> *I forgive you, God, for my abuse.*

Work with each affirmation for a week, saying it or writing it seventy times during that week. This will fulfill Jesus' teaching of forgiving "seventy times seven," which actually means to forgive continually and forever. Repeat the Forgiveness Diet as needed. This will help you to absorb the spirit of forgiveness into your very being. If you are not ready for this—and again, be patient and gentle with yourself about this—you can instead ask daily for the gift of being willing and ready to forgive. Ask your soul. Ask your God. It will be given to you in the time it is meant to happen for you, and your inner resistance and fear will melt away.

After you have practiced the Forgiveness Diet seventy times seven times for at least one month, reflect on what has changed inside you.

How do you feel different?

How do you see your abuse differently?

What do you feel towards your abuser now?

Enter into a meditation of confronting and forgiving your abuser by visualizing reading your forgiveness letter that you have been writing and speaking it to your abuser. The following is one possible meditation format to facilitate this. You can certainly create your own. It is important, though, that any such meditation include these elements: ensure that you are ready to do this and that it will be emotionally safe for you; visualize yourself supported by your God, your soul, and your soul friends—perhaps even have someone physically present when you enter into this meditation; confront your abuser with what your abuser did to you, and, without minimizing, tell your abuser how the abuse affected you; express your forgiveness; send blessing, healing and peace to your abuser. Repeat this with each of your abusers, if there is more than one.

Sit in a safe space. If you feel comfortable doing so, gently close your eyes. Focus your attention on the rhythm of your breathing. Slow and deepen your breathing. With each exhale, relax your body and let go of any tension, fear, or distracting thoughts. With each inhalation, breathe in peace, safety, and love.

When you are centered and relaxed, visualize yourself in a beautiful, comfortable environment, perhaps the safe and sacred space you developed for yourself in an earlier section. Visualize also the presence with you in this space of God, your soul, and as many of your soul friends as you desire. See and feel their presence. You are not alone. You are surrounded by love. Envision yourself wrapped in a bubble or circle of warm and soothing light emanating from each of them.

Visualize a spot in front of you at a safe distance that you will invite your abuser to sit in. Further visualize as many layers of glass walls that you think that you need between you and your abuser. Despite their thickness, you will be able to see and hear him. It is up to you if you want your abuser to see you. When you have constructed this to your satisfaction, invite your abuser to sit down in the space you have created. Know that you are in charge here and that you have made it safe for yourself.

With the help and support of your soul companions, tell your abuser that you are here to forgive him. Read your letter of forgiveness aloud to your abuser, pausing whenever you need to draw on the love and strength that surrounds you. Notice what you feel as you read the letter and what you feel after you have completed reading it.

After you are finished reading the letter, listen to anything that you imagine that your abuser may say in response. Allow him or her to apologize for abusing you, if this is what comes into your mind, and to ask for your forgiveness. If this fits, and if you are ready, accept your abuser's forgiveness and feel what this is like for you.

Take one last look at your abuser, and then say this forgiveness affirmation: "(Name of abuser), I forgive you. I bless you. I release you. May God's love, and my forgiveness, allow you to heal and become all that you are created to be."

See or hear your abuser receive this, and then safely leave.

Notice what you feel when this encounter is over. Thank all those in the circle around you who were there to support you. Affirm yourself for what you have done. Then open your eyes and record your experience in your journal.

🖊 Write a forgiveness letter to God concerning your abuse. In prayer or meditation, visualize yourself in the presence of God. You could do this on the mountaintop you visit in the Walking Meditation or in any setting that invokes God's presence for you. Read it aloud or silently to God in your prayer or meditation. Then sit in silence for a time and let God respond. What do you hear? What do you feel?

Create a forgiveness ritual that symbolizes and expresses your forgiveness and your spiritual surrender of your anger and pain. Perform the ritual alone or with your soul friends.

Forgiveness of abuse is an especially difficult process. Affirm yourself now for what you have done, and know that wherever you are on this road is blessed and is where you need to be right now. Know, too, that it is perfectly fine to leave parts of this pathway undone for now. You can return when you are ready. Look back and reflect on your journey through the Forgiveness Pathway before moving on to the next and last pathway, the Pathway of Transformation.

What has shifted or changed within you as a result of traveling the Forgiveness Pathway?

What have you learned that is vital for your healing?

What parts of this pathway will you need to revisit or complete at a later time?

What new energy or insight do you carry forward with you that will help empower you and illuminate your path?

PART SEVEN

The Pathway of Transformation

22

The Surprising Spiritual Gifts Hidden in Abusive and Traumatic Experiences

When I was young, between the ages of 5 and 25, I struggled with the speech impediment of stuttering, which at times was rather severe and debilitating. It certainly was emotionally painful. There were times too many to number when I was greatly embarrassed by my stammering speech or by my inability to speak in the classroom or in social situations for fear of stuttering over the words that I wanted to speak. I would know the answer to the teacher's question, but was terrified to raise my hand and would remain mute. I would have a joke I wanted to tell my friends, yet I kept it inside instead of risking the mortification of stuttering in front of them. I withdrew inside of my self, desperately searching to find a way to talk without the stutter and so fit in with my classmates. I was a bright, funny, likeable kid, but many people around me knew little of that side of me. They saw a quiet, shy, reserved, young man, never guessing the anxiety and shame that I lived with inside. The stuttering, which had been such a bedeviling companion for twenty years, completely left me when I was twenty-five through a healing process combining counseling and prayer that even today, feels nearly miraculous and somewhat mystifying to me.

> Love and suffering are the main portals that open up the mind space and the heart space, breaking us into breadth, depth, and communion.
> —from Richard Rohr's *The Naked Now*

I am, of course, grateful to be freed of the stuttering. I have also become grateful, though, for having been a stutterer. It was certainly painful, and it left certain emotional scars, yet I can see now how my stuttering profoundly shaped my life and character in many ways that have become total gifts. I would not be who I am and have become without the suffering that I experienced through my stuttering. Out of the pain I experienced came several gifts. Since I was forced to be quiet, I learned to listen well to others and became an excellent observer of people. In my listening, I developed the capacity to deeply feel the emotions and pain of those around me. These gifts from my stuttering days helped to make me the therapist, friend, and spouse that I grew to become. The experience of struggling mentally to find alternate words to use that I wouldn't stammer granted me a gift for words that has served me well in public speaking and writing. Perhaps the greatest grace that came from my stuttering was that it drove me inward to focus more deeply on my inner life. This became the seedbed for my inner spiritual journey, which has nurtured and guided me so well in my life. My soul used even my stuttering to draw me inward and closer to her and to God.

Love and suffering are the primary gateways to transformation of our minds, hearts, and spirits. More than anything else in life, these two vital life experiences break us open to profound personal change and life altering grace. It is easy to see how love—loving and being loved—can be so life-changing and life-enhancing. We all want that experience of love. The transformational power of suffering is not so obviously seen or desired. In fact, because we want to avoid pain, we tend to look away from it. Yet, embedded in every experience of suffering, including my stuttering and your abuse, is a seed of transformation and new life. In no way was the suffering from my stuttering the same or as severe as the suffering you endured because of your abuse. Yet, the transformation of personal suffering that I experienced with my stuttering can happen for you as well. There are graces and gifts, unpolished rough diamonds and other gems, hidden in the soil of the pain, suffering, and wounds you endured because of your abuse. They can be discovered at this point in your healing journey. They can be unearthed, polished, and displayed in ways that you could not have imagined earlier on. This is the task and challenge of the Transformation Pathway that you are now embarking upon.

> Healing does not mean going back to the way things were before, but rather allowing what is now to move us closer to God.
>
> —from Ram Dass

In some of his retreat talks, a wonderful priest friend, Father Jim Krings, now deceased, who had a rich, earthy, and imaginative spirituality, told the fable of an Irish king and his cherished diamond. This king had a small kingdom in the west of Ireland during the Middle Ages. He came into the possession of a diamond that became his great treasure. He displayed it in a prominent place in the center of his throne room. It was a large stone, with many hints of light and color, but uncut and unpolished. People came from all over Ireland to view his diamond because of its great size, and it made him famous throughout the land. The king consulted many gem cutters, but was afraid to let his stone be cut for fear of losing any of its impressive bulk.

One morning, the king entered his throne room alone and let out a great cry of anguish. When his courtiers and officials rushed in, they beheld the king on his knees before his great diamond, his eyes transfixed on a large crack that had developed in the center of the stone overnight. The crack in the very heart of the diamond looked as if it threatened to shatter the diamond into a million tiny pieces. The King frantically called for all of his diamond experts to come and examine the stone and determine how to save it. All of the kingdoms and great clans of Ireland sent their wise men and experts to help as well. But no one could figure out what to do to preserve the now-fragile gem.

One day, a mysterious, bearded man with long straggly hair and a tattered robe, a monk and storyteller from an obscure monastery on one of the rocky islands off the coast of Ireland, came into the king's court. The wild-looking man stood silently before the diamond for the longest time, looking deep into its center. He wordlessly, slowly walked around it several times, his deep-set, God-haunted eyes fixed on the crack. All in the court grew silent, wondering who this strange monk might be. Finally, the monk turned to the king and spoke, "I can save your diamond. But you must leave me alone with it for the next three days without any interruptions."

At first, the king was furious, "How dare you barge into my court uninvited and presume to tell me you can fix my stone when so many wise men have tried in vain! I do not know you. How can I trust you with my diamond?" The monk responded only with silence and a deep, piercing, and, some say, saddened gaze directed straight into the eyes of the king. The king, not used to being looked upon in this way, fell silent as well. Finally, the king, in a combination of desperation and unaccustomed surrender, relented and gave the monk permission to try to save the great stone. He cleared the throne room and left the still silent monk alone with his cherished diamond.

The three days passed very slowly for the king. He was filled with dread and grave misgivings about his decision to allow the monk to work alone on his stone. But he had made his vow to allow the monk to try and save his precious treasure, so he anxiously and prayerfully waited the three days in his private chapel. At the end of the third day, the king almost timidly knocked at the door of the throne room and asked to come in. The monk unlocked the door and wordlessly led the king into the room. The king gasped and fell to his knees. There before him catching all of the light of the dying day was a magnificent, glittering crystal diamond rose artfully cut by the monk from the king's unpolished stone. The king stayed on his knees in awe. Then the real miracle became apparent to him. The monk had somehow, mysteriously, ingeniously, shaped and carved the crack, which had once threatened to destroy the diamond, into the very stem of the gemstone rose, a crystalline stem that now held the rose up firmly into the light.

The moral of the story and the miracle of transformation is that your soul can take even the deep wound of your abuse and shape it, indeed transubstantiate it, into a great and beautiful gift for you and for others. I understand that it takes a tremendous leap of faith to accept that your so painful experience of abuse may in the end be a gift. Yet in my own life, and in the lives of many of our clients, we have found it to be so. Your abuse is not only a wound to be healed, but, through the inner work of your soul, it is also a gift to be opened. In fact, it is your very abuse wound, as with the crack in the king's diamond, that can become the center and core of your spiritual transformation and soul strength. It can ultimately be experienced as blessing! This is in no way to say that it was a good thing that you were abused. It was not. It is not to say, either, that your soul or God wanted you to suffer abuse in some sort of twisted plan to improve you. They did not. It is to declare from our belief and experience that your soul and your God can bring forth goodness, grace, and life-giving psychological and spiritual gifts even from such an unwanted and devastating curse as trauma and abuse.

Early in my career as a psychotherapist, I occasionally attended open AA meetings to better understand 12 Step recovery and spirituality and to know what some of my clients were experiencing. I was very surprised and at first puzzled to hear some of the more veteran recovering alcoholics introduce themselves as "gratefully recovering alcoholics." I came to realize that they were saying not only that they were grateful to their Higher Power for their sobriety, but also for being alcoholics in the first place. Their spiritual program in AA had brought them to the place where they could see and believe that their alcoholism, despite all the pain and damage that it had caused in their lives, was ultimately a gift. They were happy and grateful for what they had learned and for who they had become, especially spiritually, as a result of being alcoholics and traveling the road of recovery. The once shameful, destructive, and debilitating disease of alcoholism had been transformed into a blessing for them. This can become true for you as well in regard to your abuse. It too can become, in the end, a blessing for you.

Helen captures this transformation of abuse into blessing and gift in her letter to her abuser:

> While I can list all of the things that you robbed me of, I can also list the gifts that came from that experience. I have developed a sixth sense of knowing when something is not right, and that has served me well for the most part. I developed a heightened sense of my surroundings. I hear and see things that others often don't, or disregard. Even being able to dissociate from something has turned into being a gift at times. This ability has allowed me to minister to the sick in ways that I didn't know I was capable of. As a teacher, I had the gift of knowing the students that would often go unnoticed. I could see the signs of abuse in their demeanor, their spoken language, and their body language. I understood that part of them that they felt nobody else did. As a spiritual director,

this gift has evolved in a way that I am able to listen to women share their abuse experiences. I grew to be compassionate rather than angry, closed up, and resentful.

What are the gems, the gifts of spirit and character that are hidden in your experience of abuse? What have you gained, what have you learned, how are you stronger because of your abuse? Who are you now—that you could not have been otherwise—precisely because of your abuse? What inner wisdom, strength, creativity, or awareness has come from your abuse? How has your abuse broken you open to a deepened and expanded spiritual journey that might never have occurred without the abuse? What is your soul bringing forth from the depths of your suffering and woundedness that can awaken new light and life in your spirit?

These are the challenging, spirit-mending, and soul-expanding questions of the Transformation Pathway. Your answers to these questions, and the discoveries that you make within yourself about them, will be a final and perhaps surprising part of your healing journey. The previous pathways will have prepared you to listen to your soul in a way that will open up your awareness to see your abuse in a new and transforming light. The grace that you discover at the heart of your abuse experience will be a key to completing the journey from victim, to survivor, to transformed and transforming thriver. It will be your final victory over your abuse. As always, your soul yearns to speak to your heart and now to reveal to you what is being resurrected and given to you from the pain and suffering of your abuse and trauma. You are invited to open your mind and heart, receive, and be transformed.

 *Way Station*

🖋 Again enter into the Walking Meditation. This time, load your backpack with your questions about how your abuse might be transformed into spiritual gifts for you. Write your questions or hunches ahead of time. When you reach the top of the mountain, present them to your soul or the spiritual being you have been encountering. Listen to what you are told, and receive what gifts or graces from your abuse you are offered. Put them into your backpack, and then open them on the mountain, in the forest, or on the beach on the way down. Examine them. Look at them from all angles and in different light. Embrace and cherish them. Notice what you feel in receiving these gifts. When you have completed the meditation, record your experience in your journal.

🖋 Re-read the list of your losses that you developed in the Way Station in

Chapter Fifteen. Bring it to prayer and meditation, and let your soul help you to see the spiritual gifts that have come from them and from other aspects of your abuse. Rewrite the top ten losses on the left side of a piece of paper, and then write what gifts have or might emerge from them on the right side of the page opposite each loss. Notice what you feel when you have completed this. Bring this feeling to your next meditation or prayer session.

You can also do the same process with the inventories of spiritual wounds in Part Two, including The Spiritual Laundry List. Write a list of the most damaging spiritual wounds from your abuse. Again present them to your soul, and see what is revealed to you about how these wounds have now been transformed for you and what gifts have been brought forth from them by your soul. Write down the gifts and transformations that you have been given on the page opposite the wounds.

Journal

Spiritual gifts from your experience of abuse or trauma? This idea may seem absurd or even offensive to you. Vicki's journal entry below, about her journey on the Pathway of Transformation, provides some answers about how this became true for her and how it is indeed possible for you as well.

From Vicki's Journal—

The quality of any fine gem is always measured by the number of facets it exhibits. There are many facets of transformation throughout my healing process: my friend, who led me to such a gifted therapist; my therapist, who listened patiently to my story of betrayal and pain, and then led me to self-discovery I could not have imagined; my family and circle of friends, who listened patiently and supportively and helped me grieve; Mother Teresa and her community, who unknowingly created an opportunity for service that brought stability and empowerment amidst the disorder in my life; and the poor themselves, who helped put my suffering into perspective and challenged me to recognize anew the real gift of my life.

One of the earliest transformational experiences, which also became a first paradigm shift in me, occurred when I went to India to work with Mother Teresa's community. At age 24, the abuse was in its sixth year. Even then, I knew something had to change. I had begun to read about Mother Teresa in the first book about her, Something Beautiful for God by Malcolm Muggeridge, and felt called to experience her work with the poor in India. Despite pleas from my family not to go to India, I persisted in my pursuit of this goal. Painting houses to raise money to travel, I could not be dissuaded from going. Nothing could have prepared me for this experience with the poor or with the Missionary of Charity Sisters. This transforming experience would lay the groundwork for the rest of my life and truly inform all of my pursuits in the realm of spirituality, faith, and ministry. I could never have imagined the commanding influence this experience would have on the rest of my life.

After my journey to India, I became involved with the Co-Workers of Mother Teresa, a lay movement she created to support the work of her community around the world. Over time, wherever the Sisters created houses, lay people became involved in working with her Sisters to minister to the poorest of the poor. This involvement not only put me in touch with a network of like-minded people around the world, but it also connected me into a relationship with Mother Teresa herself. During the darkest of nights in my healing process, it was Mother Teresa who wrote to me to ask if I would become the National Link of the Co-Workers in the United States. Because of this call to serve by Mother Teresa, I was able to begin to climb out of my own story and begin to think of others. Mother will always be considered a significant person in the story of my healing.

During a recent visit to Kolkata, India, it was such a joy for me to pray at Mother's tomb, located just below the chapel where she attended Mass each day. In the chapel is a statue of Mother sitting on the floor in the usual prayer position the sisters would always find her. I had many opportunities during my ten-day stay in Kolkata to stand or kneel before the statue to thank Mother Teresa for her guidance and presence in my life.

My transformation evolved over time and, gradually, I began to see the movement of the Holy Spirit directing my life and guiding me into one life-giving experience after another. Transformation began to take deep roots in me with each passing year. Today, as I continue to be affirmed by my peers and those with whom I engage in ministry, I am more aware of how God is using me to bring a message of healing love, which is diametrically opposed to the trauma of darkness that I previously determined would forever pervade my very being.

At the end of the day, I have to acknowledge that my abuser was a catalyst that led me to a much deeper exploration of who I am. That is a million dollar sentence! Perhaps the loss of my sister and other life-altering events could have brought me to that point, but my reality is "stone-cast" and that experience of abuse by a Catholic priest led me down a path of self-discovery, healing, and recovery. I wouldn't wish the abuse on anyone in order to gain that type of self-knowledge, but it was the journey I experienced and now can recognize it for what it was. It is the authentic ME.

An unusual and unexpected opportunity presented itself to me recently. I was invited to visit a supervised residential facility for priests who have abused. I say it was unusual because I never dreamed I would be able to be in a space with one priest abuser let alone a couple of dozen. Yet when the invitation was made to me, it seemed like the next step. I viewed this as another moment of grace that was presenting itself. Challenging indeed, and yet I was confident that it was another step in the journey. I prayed for several weeks before going, and the more I reflected, the more I became comfortable with the potential encounter. On the drive to the center, there was an inner amazement that I was finding myself in this place at this time. And it was okay. That's not to say there wasn't a huge knot in my gut, but it was okay. In the end, they were a gracious group of men who were on a journey toward their own healing. And in that I could relate.

I pray that those who have abused and those who have been abused can find a path to transformation. Each is unique and presents opportunities and graces that arrive in various forms and not according to any timetable. It is only by doing the hard work of healing that any of us can find the transformation which will emerge from all the hurts that have twisted us, and eclipsed our power. It is the most difficult, but upon reflection, the most rewarding challenge of my life. There is no easy way around it. We must walk through the pain as surely as through a gauntlet. But once again, love, determination, time, and submission to grace will create an emergence like no other. It is not an ethereal reality but a steadfast surety that one's life is good and my reason for "being" is invaluable. That became my mantra throughout the healing process and is relevant to all of life's challenges.

All of humanity actively tries to avoid the painful experiences of life. We are able to disguise and bury hurts or occasionally even circumvent those that are headed our way. And there are those of us who know something is not right and begin asking questions and seeking answers. For myself, I was blind-sided by both the abuse and the years of incessant pain. Obviously, no one willingly asks for this type of personal trauma. In fact, it is our normal stance to ward off even a short-lived period of such oppressiveness. The grand irony of it all is the fact that because of the abuse, I was led down a path toward authentic transformation. Although none of us will ever achieve total transformation, we can be inspired to seek it and to make it our life's work to find it. Is this not a grace?

Suffering can make us bitter and closed to the love that is available to us every day. Or it can make us wise and compassionate and open to receive all that God holds out to us. Richard Rohr says that suffering can often take us to the inner edges of our resources. I thank God for the inner resources I could summon and for the resources outside myself, which became such an integral part of my journey toward healing and transformation.

I had the opportunity in 2009 to meet an amazing woman, Rose Mapendo, from the Democratic Republic of the Congo, who powerfully illustrates the choice to transform suffering. Rose was speaking at a national conference of Theresians in Phoenix. Her amazing story of surviving for seven months in a Congolese death camp with her nine children, including twin boys born in the camp, is truly miraculous. Near death from starvation, and after witnessing the torture and murder of her husband, Rose and her children were finally rescued by members of the United Nations. The passion with which Rose told her story of surviving such a horror and her willingness to understand its meaning gives great witness to the power of forgiveness and transformation.

Despite the incredible trauma of her situation, Rose had the wisdom and grace to name her twin sons after the two men who tortured and killed her husband. This insured that they would receive food. Rose shared that she was also motivated to name the boys after the two abusers because she did not want to live her life hating them. Her faith and trust that she and her children would survive is what sustained her. Where does that type of faith come from? How was she able to forgive, even in the naming of her twins? Rose did not have access to counseling, yet she was able to transform this horrific experience into something life giving that she then used to help other refugees from her war-torn country. To me, her story speaks volumes about the resourcefulness of human beings to overcome great, soul-wrenching trauma and to even utilize these experiences to re-shape their lives for the better. Those of us in the audience who hung on Rose's every word that day in Phoenix were ourselves transformed. At the end of her gut-wrenching story, she and her children sang for us, and all three hundred fifty of us danced with them around the room with amazing and transcendent joy.

Transformation is ongoing; it never ceases unless we choose to succumb to stagnation. Through the writings of Constance FitzGerald and a program called Engaging Impasse, I have learned that there are no final answers or total closure. Through contemplative listening, contemplative dialogue, and contemplative prayer, I can create a spaciousness that will hold all the questions and even some of the answers that surface. In this life, many questions go unanswered. This mystery confounds us and stymies our steps. However, by entering into the silence and listening for God's voice, we can find a way to hold all the questions, all the pains and sorrow, not only of our personal pain, but of the pain and sorrow of the world. We can find healing within the spaciousness created by contemplation. The challenge is to use it. The accessibility is at times illusive, but it is within our grasp. Contemplative silence is a balm to my soul. It allows me to rest in God's abiding love, and it energizes me to continue the journey one step at a time and with eyes wide open.

There is a spiritual phrase I once heard which referred to personal struggle as an unwanted grace. Today I can look at my experiences as an unwanted grace. The abusive relationship was unwanted of course. However, when I look at the grace that has come into my life because of that experience, I am deeply humbled. Never in a hundred years could I have imagined the grace that has come to me. It makes no sense to wonder what my life would have been without the abusive relationship. We live the life which is given to us. And every moment is our life. Paula D'Arcy, a marvelous spiritual writer and friend, has a wonderful way of saying, "This is your life, this is the life you have been given, this is it!"

23

Discovering Spiritual Meaning and Purpose in Suffering

In many ways, this is the most difficult section of this book to write. How can I find the words to describe to you, or have the nerve to say to you, that the unjust and undeserved experience of suffering that you have had can ultimately have great spiritual value, meaning, and purpose? Yet it can, and I must. In what way can I explain to you that, although your suffering in itself is in no way good, nor sent or desired for you by your soul or your God, your soul and your God have been using this suffering for your good and ultimately for your transformation towards becoming more fully who you were created to be. This is despite, and paradoxically also because, of the suffering you have experienced. This is the mystery of all suffering. It is painful, and the right spiritual response is to help to end and heal it. Yet it can be transformative.

Suffering is so difficult to make sense of. All spiritual traditions address the question of suffering. Although many provide partial answers, pieces of the great puzzle, none of them, in my opinion, provide a completely satisfying answer. I have been in what my mother somewhat sarcastically once dubbed as the "misery business" all of my life—as a social worker, priest, hospital chaplain, and now a therapist. My central calling has been to be a healer of suffering. As a close observer of human suffering and as a spiritual seeker, I have long sought to understand the meaning of suffering and see its purpose in my own life and

> I consider the sufferings of the present to be as nothing compared with the glory to be revealed in us.
> —from Romans 8:18

in the lives of my clients. I have sought to make sense of it, as you probably have, to find some answers, and to perhaps develop a grand unified theory of suffering that would put all the pieces of the great mystery together. This has eluded me my whole life, and I suspect it always will. This is the nature of spiritual mystery. It is a phenomenon just beyond our sight, replete with confusing and sometimes obscuring paradoxes and contradictions, yet yielding partial glimpses of an underlying light and liberating truth.

Certainly, the great spiritual traditions shed some illumination on the mystery of suffering. Let me briefly cite a few of the insights into the meaning of suffering some of the great traditions provide. In the Jewish tradition is the biblical theme of suffering as a purifying, refining force that shapes spiritual character and draws the suffering closer to God and God's ways. In Christian spirituality, Jesus' suffering on the cross, leading to his resurrection, is the means and the prototype for transforming our human suffering and woundedness into new life and freedom. The Buddha sought and discovered enlightenment, surrendering all attachment and ego, in order to break the cycle of human suffering. All of these, and many other spiritual teachings, offer us glimpses of the meaning, purpose, and way out of our suffering.

These insights have illuminated my own understanding, and, along with my experience of journeying with so many people in their suffering, have led me to several conclusions, partial answers, and glimpses about the meaning of the suffering caused by trauma and abuse. First of all, it is important to say that suffering is not a good in itself, nor does your soul or God sadistically want you to suffer for your own good. What they desperately long for and guide you towards is your healing. At the same time, God and your soul can use your suffering in the process of healing to shape and transform you into a new creation, stronger precisely because of your suffering. This is the paradox and mystery of suffering. Your suffering then becomes a gift, a precious and sacred wound. Your very brokenness becomes the road to transformation. This gives your suffering its spiritual meaning and purpose, even though the trauma or abuse that caused your suffering was unjust, unwarranted, and unwanted by you, your soul, and your God.

Starting with St. John of the Cross, a 16th century mystic, many spiritual writers have used the term "the dark night of the soul" to describe this journey through suffering to transformation. The intense suffering of abuse, along with any life experience involving strong physical, emotional, and spiritual pain, can throw you into such a "dark night." Night is scary. All of your fears and your pains are intensified at night. Your pathway through the pain has vanished in the dark. You cannot see your way through your suffering and feel lost and overwhelmed by it. God seems absent, your soul silent, and you certainly can see no value or meaning in your suffering. Your suffering, in fact, feels senseless, or worse, like some cruel joke of the universe. You cannot, while in this dark night, see or feel your soul at work in your pain. It is only later, looking back on these times when you have emerged from them, that you can see what your soul and your God were doing for you, in you, through your pain. This dark night can be experienced on any of the pathways described by this book, especially during the Courage and Grief Pathways.

The dark night is a very painful place to be, and yet it can be a healing, transforming place. It can become "a blessed night," "a terrible beauty." In the dark night, it feels like God and your soul are not present, are not at work in it, and yet they are. Your suffering is being transubstantiated into a sacrament of new life and light for you and eventually for the world. Through your suffering itself, you are being called and led into a deeper relationship with your soul and into an intimate union with your God.

For the dark night to become a blessing, though, you must let go of control of the process—so difficult for victims of abuse to do—and accept that, for a time, you are powerless to move yourself through the dark night by your own efforts alone. It is vital, too, for you to invite your soul and your God into your dark night and to give them permission to be at work in your pain. You need to do your best to trust that God and your soul are at work even though you see no sign in the moments of darkness that this is happening. Only later, looking back from a new vantage point of peace, healing, and new life, will you be able to see what God and your soul have been up to in the dark night of your suffering. Oscar Romero, the martyred advocate of the poor of El

> It is the fire of suffering that brings forth the gold of godliness.
> —from Madame Guyon, quoted in Rick Warren's *The Purpose Driven Life*

Salvador, captured in the prayer of his dark night what all of us are called to pray in times of such dark suffering: "I can't. You must. Show me the way."

You will be guided often unnoticed through the darkness. You will be shown the way through. You will be transformed. Your soul will employ your suffering and abuse itself to shape, reform, and recreate you to be even more the magnificent person of ultimate value that you were created to be. Suffering and brokenness bring you to your knees and entail a certain inner dying, yet, ultimately, they can lift you up and resurrect you into a fuller, deeper life. Suffering can break the hold of the small self, your ego, and open you to living in and from your big self, your God self, your soul. In St. Paul's words, "You are a new creation." Suffering, made redemptive by the actions of your soul, draws you back to your source. It leads you into a relation to that source in which you are reborn.

Nature gives us wondrous symbols and metaphors for this spiritual process of transformation. All plant seeds have to go through the transformative process of being buried in the earth, disintegrating, and dying in order for new life to sprout forth and produce a new plant. As Jesus says in the Gospel of John, "Unless a grain of wheat falls to the ground and dies, it remains just a grain of wheat; but if it dies, it produces much fruit." Your suffering, and especially the surrender of your small self that suffering invites, is the dying and the burying. The rising is the spiritual fruit, the new spiritual you, the larger you that is created, that emerges, blossoms, and gives glory and beauty to you and your world.

The life cycle of the salmon provides a dramatic story of the journey and travails of returning to the source. This story parallels your soul's own process of drawing you home to your source. Every salmon is born with an instinct to swim away from his home pool and stream to wander the oceans of the world and grow in strength and size. Every salmon is also born with an even more powerful instinct to eventually find its way back to its source stream and home pool where it was spawned. To return requires much effort, many hurdles, and challenges, what we might even describe as suffering. In the end, the return to source and the creation of new life necessitates the death of the salmon in order for it to pass on life to the next generation.

So it is with the suffering you've experienced as a result of your trauma or abuse. Transformation requires a difficult, sometimes painful journey with many challenges and much swimming against the current. It involves a dying of your old ways of thinking, feeling about, and responding to your abuse. It challenges you to let go of ego, let your soul and God be in charge in the midst of your dark night. Your suffering will, though, like the grain of wheat and the salmon, yield a new and wondrous spiritual harvest for your life. Your suffering will pull you more deeply inward into a profoundly more intimate relationship with your source.

The transformation that comes from your healing and from your soul's work in transfiguring your suffering as you travel the Five Pathways is described in the second half of the Spiritual Laundry List. Let's look at that together now.

 # A Spiritual Laundry List

The **Wash, Rinse, and Polish:** By choosing the spiritual healing journey, we learn that we can live our lives in a more meaningful manner; we can learn to change our attitudes, habits, and old patterns, including our old patterns of relating to our Higher Power, to find serenity, purpose, and happiness.

We learn that God is good and loving after all. We discover that our Higher Power does not possess any of the negative characteristics that we experienced in our abuser.

We learn to see our abusers as human beings, let go of the anger and bitterness we once projected from them onto our Higher Power, and choose forgiveness.

Our spiritual healing frees our will; we find that we have choices in our spirituality; we can choose to experience our spirit, our soul, and our Higher Power in new and life-giving ways.

We choose to surrender our lives and will to the God of our understanding.

We accept that we are accepted by God; we accept that we are accepted, and loved not for what we do—simply because we are!

We let go of the delusion and control of shame and perfectionism, stop "shoulding" upon ourselves, and begin to adopt personal values, which are reasonable, and lead to balance and wholeness.

Our spiritual journey includes chosen companions with whom we share our soul, and whom we allow to affirm, and challenge us.

Through a balanced program of prayer and meditation we develop an authentic and personal relationship with our God, and invite God into every area of our lives.

We discover our poverty without God, and daily live in our need of God.

We learn, and experience the gift of being in the present moment with our God and with God's creation.

We recover a child-like sense of wonder, joy, and awe about the magnificence of ourselves, and all of creation.

We develop a grateful heart, and live in thankfulness for the many gifts that we have been given, and that surround us always.

Our spirituality reveals to us that we are a person of great and infinite value; this knowledge about ourselves leads us to more fully value and love others in our life.

Our soul leads us to live in a new sense of purpose and mission that enhances and deepens our lives, and the lives of all with whom we come into contact.

Each individual who makes the healing journey will discover their own personal spiritual meaning for their trauma or abuse. There is no one answer or meaning. It will be different for different people. You can see examples from your soul companion's writings in this book. A breakthrough for Vicki came in her meeting with Mother Theresa of Calcutta when Mother Theresa suggested one spiritual meaning and purpose for Vicki's abuse suffering. Sue's journal entries describe her suffering's transformation into compassion and love for victims, and eventually even for perpetrators of abuse. Mike's reflection describes the answers he discovered in his pain. For some, the road to finding sense and significance to their suffering may be long and challenging. However long your road may be, you will wake up one morning, or awaken one prayer or meditation session, to a new perspective, a new angle from which to view your suffering, and see it for the first time. Then its meaning and your soul's purpose will finally become clear to you. The very act of unmasking that meaning will be healing and transforming for you.

Mike describes his experience of unveiling and discovering the meaning and transformation of his abuse suffering:

> *Self-renovation never really works well at first because it is so painful. The grief of loss of the "old self" ensues and the tears and inner pain get dislodged. I had to trust the process that all of this grief-laden pain would lead me through to the other side of myself only to discover for myself a spiritual power beyond my imagining. The journey within to the soul was a dark night and a long pathway into uncharted territory, but like the tomb after three days, resurrection began to emerge.*

I prayed so often with the scripture from John's Gospel, "I am the light of the world, if you believe in me you shall never walk in darkness. You will be a light for life" (John 8:12). Day and night I told the Lord I would trust his word. I sat in chapel or alone in my room to ponder the power of the words and breathe in the Lord's Light. As I held my breath, I would imagine the Light of Grace circulating throughout my entire body, regenerating me; then I breathed out the darkness of anger and placed my unknown self into his hands, into his heart. Over and over again, the Light came in, transforming my thinking, always dispelling the darkness of anger, depression, and hopelessness.

Trusting his promise, "You shall never walk in darkness," was already transforming me. I now tell the Lord in my prayer everyday, "I will never walk in darkness anymore." I have learned that what appears to be "darkness" is only an opportunity and a challenge to move ahead into new avenues of living. Faith and trust in God leads to faith and trust in oneself and others, and that is the Light that dispels the darkness of my doubt and fear.

In my healing journey, I began to find my way to authenticity, humble self-respect, and honesty. I met the man inside who was longing for so many years to overcome his fears and anger, his self-hatred and insecurities—and I liked him. For years and years before, I never knew how to find myself. In treatment, I did not always like what I saw, but my spirituality led me to see that the human spirit would heal given the discipline of daily attentiveness. The desire for an integrated life gradually began to win. My history of emotional and spiritual suicide, of self-alienation, found its safe home within my nurturing soul and soon fell to the earth and died, just as the seed dies in order to grow into a tree.

 ## *Way Station*

🍃 Read through the *Spiritual Laundry List: The Wash, Rinse, and Polish*. Which spiritual qualities and characteristics are now a part of your spirituality? Which spiritual qualities and characteristics can you see yourself growing towards? List them in your journal. From these, write a description of the spiritual person that you have become at this stage of the journey or that you can visualize becoming. Reflect on the role your suffering has played in developing these spiritual characteristics in you.

🍃 Prayerfully look back on your healing journey, including any "dark nights of the soul" that you have experienced. With the vision provided by your soul, what can you now see that your suffering has taught you? How have you changed for the better despite and because of the undeserved and unwanted pain from your abuse? Who have you become that you otherwise might not have been? How have your soul and your God used and transfigured your pain on your behalf and for your benefit? Write your reflections in your journal. If it fits for you now, also write a prayer of thanksgiving for how your suffering has been transformed and transforming.

🖎 Do the Walking Meditation. Pack your backpack with your questions about the spiritual meaning and purpose of the suffering that your trauma or abuse has caused. In your time at the top of the mountain, ask the spiritual being who meets you there for guidance and clarity about the spiritual meaning and purpose of your suffering. Make sure you record what you hear in your journal.

Journal

In this last journal entry, Sue describes the surprising and incredible transformation of her abuse into a ministry of love and healing not only for fellow survivors, but also for the very men she thought she would hate.

From Sue's Journal—

For the past 24 years, I have worked extensively with men and women, young and old, who have been sexually, physically, emotionally, verbally, mentally abused. I have heard and experienced with them such horrific traumas, such intense pain and sorrow. No words are awful or strong enough to describe their wounds from their abuse experience.

Through those years, Pat and I met with a colleague, Sister Mary Peace Howard, PhD, for peer supervision every other week with the intention to clear our baggage, our personal stuff and traumas, etc. out of the way in order to be more fully present to our clients. I will be ever grateful to Pat and psychologist Sister Mary Peace, for those ninety-minute sessions. At the time, these meetings could be challenging and even painful. Today, I am deeply grateful for each minute of our conversations. Just as it took the three of us courage, ever building trust with each other, to share our personal and professional struggles so deeply and openly, it requires the same courage of each person who desires to heal from abuse.

I have always been awed at the amazing bravery that it took for my clients to break the silence: to come forth trembling with fear and terror, to utter the truth, to share one's sacred story, to draw it, to cry it, to physically feel the sickening, angry, deeply hurting feelings, to courageously open one's minds and hearts to their own healing, to release the anger, the hurt, the terror, the loss of so many years of being able to be free to truly be who their God has created them to be—beautiful and magnificent boy, girl, man, woman of magnificent and eternal value. It takes great courage and faith also to first recognize the great wall of shame the abuse has engulfed them in, and then work, and I mean work, to release and tear down piece by piece, brick by brick, that thick wall of shame. Most of the time fearing that they'll discover more darkness, more shame, at the same time bravely learning to trust—God, the therapist, the group, and then themselves—and discovering the truth of who they are. The truth is that each and every one is God's most precious child, a beautiful man or woman of magnificent value, beautiful inside and outside.

You see, the abuse traumatizes many layers of the individual, and yet the abuse fails to touch the inner core, the inner tabernacle within, where God resides and whispers: YOU ARE MY PRECIOUS CHILD, YOU ARE LOVED, YOU ARE GOOD, YOU ARE WORTHWHILE, YOU DESERVE LOVE, YOU EXIST, YOU MATTER, YOU COUNT! YOU ARE YOU AND WOW! CELEBRATE YOU!

It has been in the past, and is today, my intention to stop the cycle of abuse. I feel called to journey with those wounded by abuse and coach them to hear God calling to them to heal, to stand on their own two feet, and to shout at the top of their lungs: "I exist, I matter, I count, I am God's precious child! I am free to be me!" The opportunity to walk with so many people through their healing journey has been a sacred privilege. Somehow God has used me, and my own healing pilgrimage, to be an instrument of healing for my clients. In this sense, my own sacred story, including the abuse chapter of my story, has been transformed in me to be of use for my clients. I am awed and very grateful for this. This was something that I was not surprised about. I sensed God would use my own abuse to bring healing to victims of abuse. What is happening now, and has been developing for the last nine years, has come as great surprise, even a shock, to me. Let me tell you the story of what and how this happened.

Through the peer supervision, as I mentioned before, I have been able to keep my intense anger at the perpetrators of abuse at bay: to talk the good talk that they too are God's wounded, traumatized in some way. Then one day, an invitation came to Pat and myself to work with priest perpetrators of sexual abuse of minors to facilitate a therapy and community building group for them. I was now challenged to literally not only talk the talk, but to walk the walk—to journey with these men on their pathway to healing.

My goodness, our bodies speak loudly. My stomach was churning, my heart burning, my body tight to the point of stiffness, my head was spinning, hearing of the invitation to counsel these men. I felt like Jeremiah when God called him to speak to the rebellious Israelites. Jeremiah replied, "Why me, I am too young?" Well, that line wasn't going to work for me! I was not too young. Every cell in my body resisted the idea of working with abusers! Every fear and anger that I had ever experienced about my own abuse and the abuse of hundreds of clients surfaced and said "NO WAY!" A part of me knew this was a great opportunity to put into practice so much of what I believed and had been teaching my clients about the healing power of forgiveness. I began to perceive a real spiritual call in this. An equally strong part of me, though, wanted nothing to do with this work or these men. I felt blocked and could not decide.

This is what worked to push the great stone blocking me aside and opened me to what God was calling me to. One day, Pat reminded me of my dream: many times, through the years, I would say to him, if only I could work with the priests and brothers who have abused, they too are wounded, they too are hurting, they too are traumatized. Interesting how my fear blocked that inner truth! Since that had been my dream, I needed now to listen and say "yes."

I then became aware of my further fear, my terror. I feared that I would literally hate these men—I mean 100% hate them—for their heinous crimes! With much prayer, reflection, and meditation, I came to a place of knowing that I was truly being called to walk the walk of what I so deeply believe in, and that is UNCONDITIONAL LOVE. I was being called to utilize sacred listening and hear the sacred and tragic stories of the men, the priests and brothers: to learn of their woundedness, of their own horrendous abuse and traumas as children; to stand on my own two feet and walk with them as they have and continue to feel the shame of their horrific actions; to cry and weep for how they have harmed their victims and their families, their fellow priests and brothers, and their church; to coach them on their paths of healing and help them discover goodness in themselves; to embrace the truth of who they are in God's eyes. Like it is for their victims, and for all victims of abuse, this is a very challenging task to embrace.

During these past nine years, I have grown through struggle and doubt to truly love these men. Please hear me clearly. I 100% hate their crimes, their abuse, and the horrific trauma and pain they have inflicted on their victims. At the same time, in listening with sacred listening to their stories of their own abuse and hearing their commitment to their recovery one day at a time and their commitment to pray each day, sometimes several times a day, for their victims and the families, I am able to see each one with spiritual vision. This is 20/20 spiritual vision, which enables me to perceive and experience the essence of who each one truly is in God's eyes. This vision allows me to say without reservation or embarrassment that I really do love each and everyone of them unconditionally as God's precious child.

24

The Purpose-Driven Survivor: Mission and Service Resurrected from the Ashes of Trauma and Abuse

When I was in graduate seminary, somewhere around 1972, a group of us seminary students, responding to the zeitgeist of the times, believed that our academic freedom was being abrogated by some of the decisions of the administration of the school. In reaction, we decided to develop our own campus protest, which took the form of three days of prayer and fasting from food—a spiritual protest to be sure, but also certainly a timorous one, since boycotting classes or marching on the administration offices would have meant instant expulsion. So boycotting eating was safer.

To end our protest and fast, we invited one of our scripture professors, a layman and a colorful character, Dr. Alan Arkin, to address us. I will never forget his words to us. We expected him to say something that would support our cause for freedom and galvanize our protest to some further action. Instead, he brought us short and challenged us to look deeper into our hearts and beyond our narrow self-interests about the issues of the time. He said that, in biblical spirituality, freedom is not primarily freedom from something; rather, freedom is for something beyond the individual self. God, he said, surely wants to free you from oppression, internal and external, but it is for a greater purpose than the restoration of your rights. You are freed from some injustice or subjugation to be sure. However, you are freed for something beyond you as well. You

> Jesus came "to serve" and "to give"—and those two verbs should define your life on earth, too... Jesus taught that spiritual maturity is never an end in itself. Maturity is for ministry! We grow up in order to give out.
> —from Rick Warren's *The Purpose Driven Life*

are freed so that you can more effectively and selflessly give, serve, and love. This, Dr. Arkin reminded us, is the ultimate spiritual purpose of freedom.

It is the final challenge of the Transformation Pathway to explore what your healing and freedom from abuse is ultimately for. Hopefully, in making this journey, you have experienced significant healing and freedom from the effects of your abuse. Prayerfully, you are freer from the fear, depression, shame, anger, grief, and spiritual corrosion that your abuse had inflicted upon you. What is this freedom and healing for? As a survivor of abuse, what is the larger purpose of your healing journey? It is no doubt meant to be a gift for you so that you can live more abundantly, intimately, and freely in the light and love of your soul. This in itself will give you new purpose and vigor for living. However, your soul seeks to bring forth a further, even higher purpose for you, arising from the pain and the healing of your abuse. As we have said before, your soul has been working in you to transubstantiate the spiritual oppression and darkness of your abuse into something life and light-giving. This is for your own sake, yet not for your sake alone. It is also for the healing and enlightenment of all those in your world. Your soul then is creating, and invites you to discover, a new and transcendent purpose for living and being as a healed survivor from abuse.

> The main question is not "How can we hide our wounds?" so we don't have to be embarrassed but "How can we put our woundedness in the service of others?"
> —from Henri Nouwen's *Bread for the Journey*

Nature again provides some images and symbols that illuminate. Nature does not waste anything. Everything gets recycled for a new purpose beyond itself. All matter gets recycled into some new matter, some new life or energy. This is the great "Circle of Life." Dung becomes transformed into fertilizer. A wounded or dying tree provides housing for owls, woodpeckers, and eventually food for insects and the earth into which it finally falls. One of my favorite nature metaphors for transformation involves a certain species of palm tree in Africa. It produces a large nut, a seed that can only sprout into new life and produce a new tree if it is eaten by an elephant. It must pass through the elephant's digestive system to be activated and then is ejected onto the ground with the elephant's copious and smelly excrement. This provides an excellent fertilized start for the new tree that sprouts from the nut. There is a seed of new life in your traumatic experience, and even the dung of your trauma and abuse, transformed in the digestive process of your healing journey, can become fertilizer for a new purpose in your life!

Another way to say this is that there is a spiritual call embedded in the heart of your healing journey. A call is an invitation, a passion, a desire, a choice, and a commitment all rolled into one. This call from your soul invites you to discover a new purpose for your life, which will use the spiritual gifts your soul has given you for service or ministry to others. Your soul is speaking to you quietly or loudly, always respectful of your freedom to choose to respond or not, calling to you to hear and discover what goodness for others can arise from your healing and transformation.

Many spiritual traditions teach that we are made for a life mission and purpose unique to each of us. The call is our experience of hearing that mission deep within us and reshaping our lives in order to serve that mission. All spiritual calls are shaped in some way by our life experiences. Your call, as a healed and transformed survivor or thriver, arises in part from your traumatic or abusive experience itself. Your soul has transformed your wounds into spiritual gifts that have been given to you for the purpose of sharing them with others who will be sent into your life. Your soul and your God want to play you and your life—even your experience of trauma or abuse—like a harp to bring beautiful and healing music to the world. This is the mission of a purpose-driven survivor.

Most spiritualities include some form of this phenomenon of call and mission. Once you have experienced a spiritual transformation and rebirth, you are commissioned to go out and share what has been given to you. Jesus sends his disciples to go forth and spread the good news of his teaching and kingdom. The disciples of Buddha felt a call to carry his message of enlightenment and freedom from suffering to much of Asia. The last step of the Twelve Steps of Alcoholics Anonymous reads, "Having had a spiritual awakening as the result of these steps, we tried to carry this message to alcoholics, and practice these principles in all of our affairs." The process of recovery from addiction is not just for the benefit of the individual addict, but involves a call and is not complete without a mission to share what has been given and to spread the word of what has been learned. A gift has been given you as a survivor of trauma or abuse, a spiritual awakening has happened in you in this spiritual journey of healing. What is your call? What is your mission to share and serve? Your answer to this call from your soul will help to give you new purpose and passion for your life. Then your healing will ripple out to all of those around you in the pond, lake, or ocean of your life.

The service or ministry that comes forth from your call as a survivor can be small, medium, or large. The size or the prominence of your mission does not matter. All of it is significant. Often, the most significant service is unseen. To paraphrase Robert Kennedy, few of us are called to direct the course of history, yet all of us have an opportunity to change a small portion of events, and it is from such "numberless acts of belief and courage" that human history is shaped and created. The little waves you create today will join with many others and swell to become larger and larger waves in the future. Whatever your call as a survivor, and however you choose to respond, the ministry of service that you derive from your trauma or abuse will add to and help to fill in the larger, even cosmic picture of what the Spirit is doing in the universe. It will nudge a little further the spiritual evolution of love and consciousness in our human history that different spiritual traditions universally call for and describe, albeit in a variety of different ways. You and your life are a necessary part of a long human and cosmic story. In Jesus' language, you will be doing your unique and individual part in spreading the good news and building the kingdom of God.

So your mission or ministry might involve any number of ways of sharing what you have been given. As you read in her journal, Sue's journey led her to start a very knowing and compassionate ministry of counseling at first to fellow survivors of abuse and eventually, surprisingly to perpetrators of abuse. Vicki's abuse journey led her into various forms of service work to the oppressed and needy around the world, from AIDS patients in the U.S., to the poor in Calcutta, India, and now to the leadership of a world-wide spiritual community of woman called the Theresians.

Listen to the call from your soul. Your soul will help you to discover your mission and purpose. It may involve some specific ministry or acts of service. It may lead you to volunteer some of your time to share something of your self, your healing, and your new freedom in a church or community service project. Or, like the 12th Step of AA, you may feel called to reach out in some way to fellow survivors of abuse, personally or through a survivor support or advocacy group. The ministry may come forth in a new way in a life role that you are already committed to. You may strive to bring a deeper compassion and care to all who cross your path in your present work. If you are a parent, your main mission may be to stop the cycle of abuse with you, to raise your children in a loving, affirming, and abuse-free family environment. You may live and act from a new heart and spirit in your marriage or primary relationship. Your work of service may have nothing to do directly with your experience of trauma or abuse. Instead, it may grow out of the spiritual attributes and strengths that emerge from your healing process and yet lead you into a ministry of service entirely unrelated to your trauma or abuse. Again, the form your mission takes does not matter. It matters only that you have listened to your soul and have let it fashion a mission and a new life purpose from the ashes of your abuse.

Becky captures her experience of healing and transformation leading to mission and new purpose in her poem:

> *Like a reed,*
> *I have been carved and chiseled bit by bit over time,*
> *Until there is nothing left.*
> *I have been hollowed from the inside out.*
> *When I thought I had nothing left to give,*
> *God used me as an instrument,*
> *To play the music of salvation, healing, and self-worth*
> *To those who were equally emptied of their spirits.*
> *And so, by the grace of God,*

I have been transformed from victim to victor.

Sue and I had a profound experience of the spiritual power of living passionately from purpose two years ago when we visited a dear friend of ours, Father Darrell Rupiper, OMI, in the hospital. Darrell, in his early 70's and still vibrant and active in his ministry, had been diagnosed a month earlier with acute leukemia. His doctors had given him a grave prognosis. They suggested aggressive treatment and held out some hope, but added that his condition could well be terminal. When Sue and I heard this, we quickly decided to drop everything, and drive several hundred miles to see our friend, perhaps to say goodbye.

We snuck a small bottle of pre-mixed margaritas and three red long-stemmed margarita glasses into Darrel's hospital room. When we opened up the smuggled bag, Darrell laughed with delight. The three of us had often met in recent years at Mexican restaurants, where we had many warm, intimate, and deeply spiritual conversations over margaritas, salsa, and chips. Although he could have only a few sips of his drink, our time with Darrell sharing margaritas and our souls felt like Eucharist, a sacramental moment of thanksgiving, celebration, friendship, and soul-to-soul communion.

Darrell talked openly with us about his prognosis. He said that he could peacefully accept it if it was his time to die. He was ready if God was calling him now. At the same time, he did not want to die yet, because, as he said with great force, "I have so much yet to do." For several decades, Darrell's passionate life purpose and mission had been to bring justice, healing, and community to the oppressed and abused of the world. He had worked with the poor in Brazil and in the U.S. and had been jailed several times for speaking out and demonstrating against the oppressive policies of several governments, including our own. His most recent passion had been to educate and advocate for environmental healing and change from a spiritual and social justice perspective. He dearly wanted to live to continue this work that he felt so passionately about.

We talked some time over margaritas about his life and ministry. We again asked Darrell to tell us the story of when he felt called to this work of justice and healing. This is what he related to us. He was working as a missionary in a very poor section of the city of Recife in Brazil. He had been out visiting parishioners when he happened upon a young woman who lived with countless others around the city garbage dump, eking out a bare, subsistence living from the cast-off food and refuse of the dump. The young mother was holding her infant child and comforting her. Darrell could clearly see that a rat had eaten one of the child's feet and knew that the child would probably die. He brought the mother and child to a clinic, begged the medical personnel for help, and then went back to his church in a fury at the horror and injustice that he had just witnessed.

He went to his room dispirited and angry. There was a crucifix on the wall of his room with the traditional small statue of Jesus hanging on the cross. He poured out his rage at Jesus, railing at him about the injustice of what he had just seen with the baby and young mother. He angrily demanded to know why and how this could happen. If God was supposedly so loving and powerful, how could such awful things happen, especially to the innocent and vulnerable? What he heard deep within him in the midst of his anguished cry changed the course of his life and drove him, over the next several decades, to live and work with a great passion and purpose for justice and healing.

Darrell told us that no words could truly capture what he heard, and felt that day before the crucifix. But the message he received in response to his angry tirade to Jesus was essentially this:

> *I know your anger at injustice. It is my anger too. I know their suffering. It is my suffering too. I carry their suffering on my shoulders here on the cross. I suffer each time someone is mistreated or abused. I want to free each one from their enslavement to oppression, and comfort each one in their sorrow. I call you and many others to be my instrument of liberation and healing. I will be with you at your side as you do my work of justice in the world.*

This spiritual encounter turned Darrell's anger into a lifetime of action for justice inspired by this call.

At the end of this story, with tears welling in his eyes and a mixed tone of frustration and sorrow in his voice, Darrell softly cried out, "If only we all really understood what Jesus is saying to us!" Sue and I were deeply moved again by the story and by this last statement and heard it as an expression and even a summary of Darrell's continued deep passion for his call and life purpose.

After this sacred moment of communion with him, we spent another hour or so walking with Darrell around the cancer floor. Darrell had been there about a week at this point. He seemed to know everyone: staff, patients, and family. As he dragged around his IV bags on a wheeled IV pole, he would stop to introduce us to different people, talk for a moment to encourage a struggling patient or family member, tease and joke with a nurse, or discuss one of the environmental pamphlets he had given to some of the staff. He was, as always, reaching out to those around him, building community, bringing healing, educating and enlightening about peace and justice for the planet. Even now, facing a desperate illness, he was living beyond himself and living his purpose. Three days later, he died of his leukemia. Sue and I still miss him greatly and yet often feel the presence of his spirit and energy.

We know that we will have heard and fully lived our purpose if, at the end of our days, we possess even a measure of Darrell's peace, passion, and generosity of spirit. Darrell died with an unbroken spirit, alive until the end, with the energy and fire of his life purpose and call still aflame in his soul. My prayer for you, and for myself, is that we may all hear and discover our call, a call that, for a survivor, will be brought forth at least in part from the healing and transformation of trauma or abuse. I pray, too, that we may then live our calls deeply and passionately each day for as many days as we are given. I pray that the end of your healing journey will be to come back to living from soul, living on purpose, and living in the Spirit, the ultimate goal and final transformation of all of our journeying through this life. Amen—so be it!

 *Way Station*

🖎 Do the Walking Meditation one last time. This time, bring nothing in your backpack. Hike up the mountain with it empty and light. When you meet your soul or other spiritual being on the mountaintop, ask for a mission and new purpose that arises in some way from your abuse and your healing journey. After you have received it, embrace it, and put it in your backpack to bring it down the mountain to the outside world. In your journal, reflect on this call and explore how you are going to put it into action in your life. If you do not at first hear a call or receive a mission, do not be discouraged. Wait for it, it will come. Keep returning to the mountain until it is given to you.

🖎 Write your mission statement. Your mission is what you will do to live your purpose. A mission statement is an expression of the purpose, passion, vision, and commitment that has grown in you as a result of your healing experience on this journey. It is the distillation and crystallization of all that you have learned and been given along the way into a short statement of how you are going to live your emerging life purpose. The mission statement includes a concise formulation of your life purpose and a brief description of your life mission. Think of this as a press release or a spiritual tweet to the world and to your self about how you intend to live your life now and in the future from your new sense of purpose.

Below is a process for creating your mission statement.

Go to the safe and sacred place that you created earlier in the book, either your inner sanctum or the sacred physical space where you go to meet your soul.

Reflect on your passage through the Five Pathways and listen to your soul speaking to you about what has become most important to you now:

What essential values have surfaced?

What have you become passionate about in regard to your life?

What vision do you now see for your life?

What have you been given that you want to share?

How would you share it?

What actions can you take to live this vision?

From your reflections and your dialogue with your soul, write a mission statement by completing the following:

My purpose as a survivor at this time in my life is…

To fulfill this purpose, the mission that I accept and commit to is…

❧ Review your progression through the Transformation Pathway in your journal:

What has changed in you and in your spirituality on this pathway?

What are the key insights that you have gained?

What new purpose and energy do you carry with you as you complete this pathway?

❧ Congratulations! Your journey is complete! Look back and reflect on your whole passage through the Five Pathways, again writing your thoughts in your journal:

What do feel now at the end of your journey?

What were the highlights of the journey for you?

How are you different now? How would you describe yourself at the beginning of the journey? How would you describe yourself now?

How are you different spiritually? What was your spirituality like before? How would you characterize it now?

If you could pick a well-known known person or fictional character to represent who you were at the start of the healing process, who would that be? Who would represent you now?

What image or symbol would best capture who you were at the beginning? What would symbolize you now?

What are the five most important realizations and changes that you have received along the way?

What parts, if any, of your healing journey remain unfinished? Do you want to return to them now or revisit them later?

Going forward, how will you live your life differently now that you have completed this journey with your soul?

❧ Create and perform a ritual of completion and healing, celebrating the end of your journey and all of the milestones and healing moments along the way. Perhaps invite your soul friends to share in the ritual so that they can celebrate with you.

❧ Write a prayer of completion and thanksgiving to your soul and to your God for your healing travel through these Five Pathways. Share it with your soul friends who have been your companions along the way. Be sure to thank them as well.

Conclusion—The Journey Complete and Ever-Unfolding: Living in the Circle of God's Love and Value

We pray—all of us who have been blessed to travel with you, Sue, Vicki, Pat, Becky, Helen, and Mike—that your journey through the Five Pathways has been healing and transformative for you. We pray that you are experiencing greater freedom from both the psychological and spiritual wounds of your abuse and that your soul's guidance through these pathways has brought you to a place of peace, serenity, joy, and deep connection with your soul and your God. We pray that this journey of healing will not end here and will continue to unfold for you in an ever-growing awareness of who you, your soul, and your God truly are. There is more, we are sure, to be healed and revealed.

In this book, we have employed the metaphor of a journey, a spiritual pilgrimage for your spiritual healing process. It is a powerful image. Healing is a journey. Indeed, life itself is a pilgrimage of soul. Yet there are limitations to this metaphor. It unfortunately and mistakenly implies that there is an end, a destination to your journey, and that once you are there, you have arrived and need to travel no more. The imagery of journey also tends to focus awareness on a past that you have come from and a future you are heading toward. This can distract you from the spiritual power of simply being mindful in each sacred moment of your life, being present to the now so many spiritual writers call us to.

> At the still point, in the center of the circle, one can see the infinite in all things.
> —from Chuang Tzu, 4th Century BC Chinese Tao Philosopher

In fact, the journey of spiritual healing and transformation that we have been describing has no end. You will never cease to travel its roads and its pathways. The "destination" is an ever-deepening dance and union with your soul and with God. There is actually no past or future on this journey. Every journey of the soul, indeed every life, is really a series of nows strung together like a string of "pearls of great price," one sacred, precious, eternal moment after another. The spiritual challenge is being fully aware and fully present to each moment of your life and, in each moment, being alive to the blessing that God and your soul are offering. This is the actual destination of your journey. Yet it is not a destination at all. It is a movement, a dance led by your soul with and towards God. It is a dance ever-unfolding from one eternal Now to the next.

There is a saying, "Wherever you go, there you are!" A key to living your life's journey with serenity and joy is the capacity to know and live who you truly are. It is the awareness that your soul, your spiritual essence, your True Self is who you actually are. It is the knowledge that because of this, you, all of you, are of inimitable and infinite value and worth, and nothing—including trauma and abuse—can add to or subtract from that value. It just is. If you carry this awareness with you wherever you go, whatever you experience, then where you are in each moment, and whatever is happening to you in that moment, is a blessing. We call this living in the circle of value. Living each day in the circle of value, the circle of God's eternal love for you, in each now of your life, is our ultimate goal for your healing journey. It is our goal for our selves as well.

Living in the circle of value means abiding in and living from your center, your soul, no matter where your life's journey brings you. It means knowing that your soul is your True Self and that nothing can diminish, tarnish, or separate you from your True Self, so nothing can rob you of your magnificence and worth. It is defining yourself not by any external surface measures of self-image or self self-esteem, but by the image of God that you were created to be and by the soul-esteem your soul bequeaths to you just because you are you. It is, therefore, living from an inner sanctuary free from any fear or shame, in the complete knowledge that you are loved and sustained by infinite love and that love will never forsake you. And it is, in the inner sanctuary of the circle of value, understanding that your very essence is such that it cannot be harmed, abused, controlled, or shattered, and is already—even if secretly—perfect .

> Say not, "I have found the path of the soul."
> Say rather, "I have met the soul walking upon my path."
> —from Kahlil Gibran's *The Prophet*

Abiding in the circle of God's love and your soul's value frees you from having to fight through life to defend your small self, your fearful, limiting ego. There is no need. You are not that little self. You are a magnificent person of infinite value. No one, no thing, and no event can take that from you. You can, therefore, live in and from your big self, your True Self, your soul. Living in the circle means you can enjoy the externals of your life and the characteristics of your persona in the world, but do not have to be defined by them or work so hard to shore them up and protect them. You no longer need to expend and waste so much psychic energy in the psychological self-defense of enhancing and protecting your self-image in the world. You live from an interior sense of what Beatrice Bruteau, in *Radical Optimism*, calls "I am, I am here, I am now, I am I"—and "I am a person (always and everywhere) of magnificent and infinite value."

Living in the circle frees you, then, to live from your Truest Self. It frees you to be the individual word that is spoken with and by the Eternal Word. You exist in the formless world of soul, since that is who you are, and yet are freer to live peaceably in the world of material form. You are capable of being at home in many places because you have a home deep within yourself, your inner sanctuary of communion with your soul and with God. You then can be at home always with yourself and know that you are never alone in anything. You experience yourself to be the dance of the "Great Dancer" as you make and create your own unique moves and steps in the dance of life. You are co-creating yourself with your Creator. As you learn to live in the circle of value, to live in the truth of who you truly are, you unite yourself ever more fully with your soul and with God, "the Absolute Ground of Being." As Rodney Smith says in *Stepping out of Self-Deception*, you "join it in being and doing what it is being and doing," which means being and doing love.

The image that occurs to me to describe what living in and from the circle of value entails and promises comes from my iPhone. Its Maps App, which can help me navigate anyplace in the world, employs a GPS function which tells me exactly where I am any place on the planet and, from my location, gives me directions to wherever I want to go. The icon for my current location is a blue point of light with a blue circle of light pulsing and radiating out from it to the surrounding real estate I happen to be in at the time. Theoretically, I can never be lost because I always know where I am.

The point of light is your soul. The pulsating light emanating from the point is your own circle of God's love and value that always surrounds you. Living in the circle of value, you can never truly get lost because the GPS of your soul will always tell you where—and more importantly who and whose—you are. You have only to hit the search button for your soul to activate your inner point of light and your circle of value. You will find your way, then, in each moment. This is what centering prayer and meditation and the other spiritual practices you have developed on the Pathways can be for you. They are your "search buttons" to reconnect you with your soul in the center of your sacred inner circle, so that you can always be guided on your journey.

One hot summer's day, I was away, writing at a hermitage cabin at Windridge Solitude in the countryside outside of St. Louis. I looked up from my computer and out the front window to see a remarkable sight. There was a line of about twelve red stepping-stones stretching from the front door of the cabin, leading through the grass to the main road that wound through the retreat center grounds. On each stepping-stone, several small butterflies had alighted and were, except for the occasional flapping of their wings, sitting very still. There were five or six species of these tiny butterflies of all different colors scattered in small groups on the stones: blue, orange, green, yellow, brown, spotted, and striped. There appeared to be fifty or sixty butterflies on the whole of the path outside my window. They were each so small, though, that it would have been easy not to notice that they were there at all. Together, they made a rainbow path of tiny vibrant bits of color starting at my front door and leading out to the road and the outside world.

Butterflies are, of course, one of nature's great symbols of transformation. Their life cycle from caterpillar—sometimes rather ugly—to the cocoon and chrysalis stage, to eventual emergence as a colorful, evocative image of new and winged life is a metaphor for what is possible for each of us spiritually. The phenomenon before me that day reminded me that each moment in our journey, each step of the way contains butterflies of many colors, varieties, and sizes, all possibilities for us to transform and fly. We need only the light of our souls, shining forth from within our circles of value, to see them. Our final prayer for you, and for every survivor caught in the pain and darkness of abuse, is that your ever-unfolding path will be full of butterfly moments on each step of your continued journey. We pray that, one step at a time, in each of your now moments along your life's way, you will continue to experience new life, beauty, joy, the freedom to fly and soar high above the abuse, and ever abide in the deep serenity of your unbroken spirit and of your undefiled and eternally one and perfect soul.

Index

Recommended Resources

Any healing journey from the psychological and spiritual wounds of abuse and trauma is a journey best done with helpful and supportive companions. It does not have to be, and should not be, done alone. Today, we are blessed with many local, regional, national, and international resources for survivors of all kinds of abuse and trauma. They include support groups, support organizations, counselors, pastors and spiritual directors, retreat and treatment centers. We provide here a limited list of such resources that we are most closely connected to in order to help you find the most helpful companions for your journey to wholeness in body, mind, and spirit. You will find similar resources in your own community and network.

12 Step Support Groups

- SIA – Survivors of Incest Anonymous – www.siawso.org
  410-893-3322
- CoDA – Co-Dependents Anonymous – www.coda.org
  888-444-2357
- Al-Anon (especially ACA (Adult Children of Alcoholics) meetings)
  www.al-anon.alateen.org – 888-4AL-Anon (425-2666)

Hotlines and Support Organizations

- RAINN – Rape, Abuse, Incest, National Network - www.rainn.org
  800-656-HOPE
- ASCA – Adult Survivors of Child Abuse –www.ascasupport.org
- Office of Child and Youth Protection – U.S. Catholic Bishops – Victim Assistance Coordinators – www.usccb.org/ocyp
- Pandora's Project – rape and sexual abuse – www.pandys.org
- www.isurvive.org - on line support community for survivors
- Institute on Violence, Abuse, and Trauma – www.ivatcenters.org
- National Domestic Violence Hotline – www.thehotline.org
  800-799-SAFE (7233)
- Suicide Hotline – 800-SUICIDE (784-2433)

Professional Resources

- Spiritual Directors International – www.sdiworld.org
- Spiritual Directors and Retreat Centers – www.findthedivine.com
- American Association of Christian Counselors – www.aacc.net
- Society for Advancement of Sexual Health – www.sash.net

About The Authors

Patrick Fleming is a psychotherapist and personal coach specializing in the treatment of abuse and trauma, sexual addiction and compulsivity, couples counseling, and the integration of spirituality and psychology. Shattered Soul?: Five Pathways to Healing the Spirit After Abuse and Trauma is his second book. Previously, Fleming co-authored Broken Trust: Stories of Pain, Hope, and Healing from Clerical Abuse Survivors and Abusers. He has been a parish priest, a hospital chaplain, workshop presenter, a hospice counselor and a psychotherapist for twenty-seven years, and lives in St. Louis, MO, with his wife and co-author Sue.

Sue Lauber-Fleming is a psychotherapist and personal coach specializing in working with survivors of emotional, physical, and sexual abuse. She has been a mental health nurse, hospital chaplain, and workshop presenter. Shattered Soul? is her second book. Previously, Lauber-Fleming co-authored Broken Trust. She has raised five wonderful children and is the proud grandmother of ten, and great-grandmother of two. She lives in St. Louis, MO, with her husband and co-author Pat.

Vicki S. Schmidt has been involved in missionary outreach work since her early teens. Since 1999, she has served as Executive Director of Theresians International, a global Catholic women s organization founded in 1961 in Pueblo, Colorado. Schmidt lives in Springfield, Illinois.

CPSIA information can be obtained at www.ICGtesting.com
Printed in the USA
LVOW130949301012

305035LV00001B/27/P